INDIGO AWAKES

Stephanie
de Winter
xx

INDIGO AWAKES

One woman's journey
from abuse to spirituality

Stephanie de Winter

A record of this publication is available from the British Library.

ISBN 978-1-907203-44-2

Typesetting by Wordzworth Ltd
www.wordzworth.com

Cover design by Titanium Design Ltd
www.titaniumdesign.co.uk

Printed by Lightning Source UK
www.lightningsource.com

Cover image by Anne Sophie Roux

Published by Local Legend
www.local-legend.co.uk

To my wonderful children Tara and Krystian,
to my mother Kay and to the memory of
my father Frederick and his blue typewriter.

Acknowledgements

Thank you, Kay Johnson, for your encouragement over the years and for taking so much time to read and edit this book.

I also thank English teachers Liz Witham and Betty Cavendish for their positive input, Jill Allen and Professor Peter Merchant for believing in my ability, my cousin and friend Paul Connolly who inspired me without knowing it, Nigel Peace at Local Legend for his advice and for believing in me, and Stephane Burton, my Reiki Master and friend, who saved me during a time of crisis.

About the Author

Stephanie de Winter writes from her home in East Lothian where she lives with her two children. She has recently discovered Reiki and is learning the art of spiritual healing.

Indigo Awakes is her debut novel and she is now writing a sequel.

Contents

ONE

Going Nowhere

Screams of terror ripped through the darkness. Indigo awoke with a start. An icy chill shot through her. The screaming was high-pitched and primitive. Jerking upwards, she attempted to sit up, desperate to awaken fully; but something had hold of her hair, tugging it, pinning her to the bed. The shrill sound intensified. Fear gripped her in its vice-like skeletal clutches, shooting to her bowels. Her ears and throat hurt and suddenly she realised that the dreadful screams were her own. The digits of the clock glowed red in the darkness reading 4 a.m. and, as realisation dawned, the screams ceased.

Sense prevailed. Another nightmare had visited her and she had been lying on her long dark hair. Wriggling from the constraints of her restless sleep, she flicked on the side light, staring manically into the glow. Clammy skin saturated in a cold sweat, her wild hammering heart beating at an explosive speed. Feeling battered and exhausted, she lay back on the soft white plump pillows like a convalescing patient, allowing her mind to drift back to the dream that had terrified her.

◆ ◆ ◆

It had been night-time and the sky was a dark midnight blue. A smattering of wispy clouds partially blocked the half-moon from time to time. Indigo was running along a path at the side of a field near her home. Dark green leaves rustled to her right and silver

1

prickly barbed wire glinted in the moonlight to the left. The field was full of shadowy black horses and she could feel energy surrounding her. A sensation began to build in her hands, initially the size of a tennis ball, like a huge force swelling, growing larger. It was as though she was cupping something powerful. Frightened, she glanced behind her. Something was following her, chasing her. A presence that she couldn't see but knew was there.

She awoke with a start, or so she thought, but couldn't find her lamp. Leaping out of bed, she rushed to the main light switch on the far wall. Turning, Indigo saw herself lying in bed fast asleep, pale and peaceful but empty of life-force, with long dark hair spread over the white pillowcase. For a moment she felt upset that she'd died and a sinking feeling of disappointment engulfed her. She hadn't done half the things she wanted to do yet. Indigo wasn't ready to die. A practical calmness descended telling her that she was in the wrong place and should return to her body. She tiptoed back to the bed.

◆ ◆ ◆

She awoke properly this time, screaming. In the dream she had been calm about the out-of-body experience, but her waking consciousness had a different perspective on it.

The darkness of the night outside enveloped the safety of her lit cocoon and she lay inside the brilliant white bubble feeling exhausted. These frequent nightmares had left her feeling tired, restless and anxious the next day. However she'd always been able to put them to the back of her mind and carry on with the monotony of daily life. But this experience had been different and it really bothered her. Seeing herself lying there, still fairly young and beautiful, but dead, had disturbed her. Obviously she'd soon realised that she was alive but those few seconds had made an impact.

Mike's side of the bed was cold and empty like their relationship. Mike, her partner of the last four years, had gone to a poker night. The group of friends met every other Thursday in Ashford, playing cards, drinking huge quantities of whisky, before staggering back to the four-bedroom bachelor pad belonging to Jeff, one of the players. But Indigo was relieved by the break from him. She'd moved in with him three months before and regretted the decision almost daily. During that time she learned that Mike was not an easy man to live with. He drank heavily in the evenings which made him argumentative and he often fell asleep in front of the television. He was moody, either grumpy or abstracted but seldom cheerful. His feelings of jealousy had increased with frequent and unreasonable accusations. However, there was an adjustment period for couples moving in together for the first time. Indigo was determined at least to try and adjust.

Her mobile `phone bleeped as she rushed up the steps of the tall impersonal grey office building where she had worked for the past year. Situated down a side road just off Canterbury town centre, it was a convenient location. Umbrella and handbag in one hand, she rummaged through the hidden depths of her leather bag searching for her `phone. The sky darkened and rain began to pelt onto her umbrella, ricocheting off the ground and soaking her ankles and feet.

"Hi Babe. Meeting friends down from Yorks tonight in town for dinner. Fancy it?"

"Good God," Indigo said out loud.

They rarely socialised with his friends, especially the ones from his home town in Yorkshire. He said he preferred to spend time alone with her. Indigo re-read the text. Yes, she had read it correctly. Apprehension gripped her. What if she had nothing to say to anyone, or they thought that she was dull or ugly? She had been desperate to be integrated into his circle of friends, but now that it was finally happening she wasn't sure if it was what she wanted. Indigo's mind scanned the contents of her wardrobe. She'd wear something sexy but sophisticated. Her little black dress with black platform shoes and her ruby fake fur jacket.

On the upside, her volatile employer Jeremy Clifford-Amos was away for a week on holiday, sunning himself in Spain with his latest girlfriend. Therefore there would only be the two of them in the office. Jeremy would be expecting an email from her at 8.55 a.m. wishing him good morning. It was already three minutes late. Running up the stairs, she burst into the office. Janey, the quantity surveyor, was at her desk pouring over architectural plans, pencil in one hand and ruler in the other.

"Hi, Janey."

Rushing to her desk she flicked on the computer, tapping the desk impatiently waiting for it to start.

"You shouldn't let Clifford-Amos bully you." Janey re-tied her long blonde hair back into a pony tail.

"I know how to deal with the likes of Jeremy Clifford-Amos."

"So I see." Janey smiled. "I'll make you a nice cup of coffee while you send morning greetings to our lovely chairman."

"Thanks, you're an angel." Indigo slumped behind the computer screen.

Opening her email account, a message screamed out from Jeremy Clifford-Amos.

"You're late Indigo. If this happens again you will receive a written warning. I'll be talking to you upon my return. Not bloody good enough!"

She deleted it.

Indigo took a sip of her coffee and re-read the message from Mike. He would be expecting an answer. Images of the dream kept flashing through her mind. It had left her with mixed feelings. Nightmares were the norm for her. Her nights had been full of them as a child. The sensation of energy in her hands wasn't new either. But the feeling of being hunted by an evil presence had been petrifying. She felt battle-worn; even her nights were full of struggle. A light of realisation flashed for a split second, as a thought flitted through her brain. It was a sense of enlightenment relating to Mike. She tried to grab hold of it but the next second it was gone. The `phone rang and the thought fled.

She must make every effort to save her relationship. It was important to live life to the full. This included going out with Mike and his friends when she didn't feel like it. Indigo sighed at the thought of it. She felt tired but restless. Thinking ahead to the evening, she would rather curl up alone in her own house with a glass of wine and a good film. The heavy clutching feeling of foreboding lay in the pit of her stomach. She wasn't sure if she loved Mike or not. He was highly critical of her. Nothing she did was good enough, and her confidence and self-esteem were decreasing by the day. Deep within her, she knew their relationship was flawed, but she was in denial.

They had met on an Internet dating site and emailed each other several times over the Christmas break. He had spent Christmas in Mexico, alone. She should have known then that he was different to other men. Upon his return they met in a coffee shop in Canterbury High Street. She remembered the meeting well.

She had been sitting waiting, pretending to be cool and confident when really her insides were churning with nerves. Mike had been forty-nine at the time, twelve years older than her. Several older men had walked into the café, and she had sat there thinking 'No, not him,' and 'Phew, not him'. Suddenly a very attractive fit man with light brown hair walked in, exuding charisma and confidence. He walked straight up to her, put his arm around her shoulder and kissed her on the cheek.

"Hi, Indigo, I'm Mike. How are you? Can I get you anything, another coffee?"

Indigo remembered feeling both relieved and thrilled as she looked up into his twinkly blue eyes. She noticed how he chatted to everyone as he queued up for his drink, making a special effort to make the elderly ladies in the line laugh. She also saw how other women looked at him. He was full of charm and energy.

They agreed to meet for dinner the following weekend. They were intellectually matched, and the sexual chemistry between them was quite over-powering. The relationship was new and exciting for the first month until Mike's fiftieth birthday loomed. It soon became apparent that his ex-girlfriend was heavily involved in the arrangements for his party and it was also obvious that Indigo was not invited.

"Chrissie's involved with the family. I was with her for seven years, and they've been planning this for ages."

The party was to be held in the north of England, in Yorkshire, near to where his mother lived.

"So I'm not invited?" Indigo had finally summoned the courage to ask.

"I can't just turn up with some mystery woman I've only known for five minutes. I'll not expose you to that crowd."

Indigo recoiled with hurt, especially as they'd just finished making love in her bed. In addition, when they woke up the following morning, Mike received a `phone call from Chrissie asking what time he was picking her up.

"Yes, I'm giving her a lift. Look, I didn't want to do this sort of thing anymore but she's travelling up with me, that's all. What's the problem?"

Indigo believed what she wanted to at the time. They split up shortly afterwards, but time is a healer. When enough time passed for her to forget how hurt she'd been, Mike got back in touch. He persuaded her to meet him for dinner and plied her with charm, wine and sex and this was the pattern for their future.

TWO
Descending

Indigo made a special effort that evening to impress Mike and his friends from Yorkshire. Applying another layer of mascara, she sprayed herself with perfume and brushed her hair. She looked good. Slipping on her black high heels she walked out of the dressing room.

"Wow, you look nice," he said, smiling. He was standing in the bedroom putting on his Rolex. "Really nice. Hmmm..." he growled softly. Stroking her bottom he pushed her back onto the bed.

"I've just done my hair," Indigo protested.

Mike's face darkened.

"You're usually not bothered about your hair? Why tonight?"

Indigo couldn't face a row. If she didn't have sex with him he would cause a scene and then the evening would be spoilt.

"Just wanted to look nice for you, that's all,"

"Did you now..." he murmured seductively.

Kissing her, he pulled up her dress. A few moments later he had finished and she was back in the dressing room wiping off smeared lipstick and re-applying make-up. Her hair was dishevelled despite brushing it but it suited her.

Indigo climbed into his silver Aston Martin and he ran his hand up the length of her leg.

"Cheeky," Indigo slapped his hand playfully.

"See, your hair's not mucked up. You look like the little one from that programme with the women, you know, in America." He was in a good mood now.

"Desperate Housewives?"

"Yes, what's her name?"

"Eva Longoria. Surprised you watch that?" Mike was more of a football or politics type of man.

"Watched a bit the other night, after you'd gone to bed... There was nothing else on. Except that you have different eyes. What colour are yours?"

"Indigo. Or black, depending on my mood!"

You can hardly miss them, she thought crossly. Her eyes were vivid indigo, and her best feature. She couldn't believe he'd had to ask her after all the times they'd made love and he'd hovered over her staring into her eyes. How could he do that and not even notice what colour they were? Mike was dressed in black trousers and a purple shirt that complemented his colouring.

"Your shirt brings out the colour in your lovely blue eyes," she said pointedly. He smiled, but clearly missed the point.

"You won't say anything that embarrasses me, will you?"

"What do you mean?"

"Well, Lynn's always disapproved of me. You know that. She thinks everyone should be married with kids. Just don't want you telling her anything personal about me or us."

"Why would I? No, of course I won't," replied Indigo. A flush rose to her cheeks. That was insulting.

"I'm going to leave the car in the car park," he said abstractly. "Then I can have a drink. Pick it up tomorrow."

Entering the Moroccan restaurant, the smell of incense and exotic spices hung in the air stimulating the appetites of the hungry diners. It was open plan with dark wooden floors. Red textured wallpaper and colourful patterned rugs hung from the walls. Lanterns and candles illuminated the surroundings. The eating areas contained low tables with cushioned benches packed full of diners of all ages from teenagers to business people. Belly dance music strummed in the background. Two couples waved to Mike.

"Over here."

Both girls looked surprised by Indigo's appearance but in that slightly taken aback way that women have when faced with an attractive woman. Indigo had never seen a photograph of Mike's ex-girlfriend and their reaction made her wonder what she had looked like.

"Sorry we're late. We had a few last minute things to do..." said Mike, winking. "Indigo, this is Sarah and Tom. Meet Indigo, everyone."

"Hi," they chorused.

Sarah was about thirty-five and attractive with green eyes and long brown hair. Her partner Tom was about the same age as Mike, a little overweight with bad skin but a kind face. He was a fireman and she was a single mum.

The other couple were Glen and Lynn. He ran a successful scrap business and she didn't work. Glen was very friendly and natural, with clear blue eyes and grey hair. Lynn was in her late forties. She shook Indigo's hand weakly, and although she smiled Indigo could tell by her eyes that she had taken an instant dislike to her.

Mike whispered in Indigo's ear.

"Sarah's wearing a little dress too. Looks like you wore the right thing."

Indigo looked at him incredulously. What on earth did he think of her to make such strange comments? Did he think of her as a tramp or was he just chronically insecure? Not bothering to answer, she took a gulp of red wine.

"So, have you got any children?" Sarah asked as the main dishes arrived. Mike topped up their wine glasses.

"Yes, two. They're nineteen and twenty-one. Both at Leeds University actually."

"Oh really? What do they do there?"

"Charlie's doing Theatre and Lily English."

"Oh, that's good."

"Cor... she's nice," Mike murmured to Glen across the table.

Glen looked startled and embarrassed. Glancing at Indigo he said to Mike quietly:

"Mate, look who you're with."

"Just saying that she's extremely good-looking."

Mike was referring to one of the waitresses, a tall and slim, pretty girl aged about twenty. Indigo raised her eyes to heaven and took another slug of wine. The next moment the volume of the music increased and a belly dancer of about thirty glided over to their table and began swaying to the music, circling her hips and waving her arms in the air. She was very sensual with a good covering of flesh.

9

"Indigo can belly dance," Mike offered.

"I don't think it's me that she wants to dance with, do you?" Indigo said loudly with a wicked gleam in her eye.

"Yeah, come on mate, up you get." His friends entered into the spirit.

Mike got up and moved his hips stiffly in front of the belly dancer, putting his arms up as if he'd danced like this on his travels when he'd been a younger man. Everyone clapped when he sat down and she moved on to the next table.

"Put your napkin on your lap dear," said Indigo.

"Her? You must be joking. Too fat. You on the other hand...." Under the table, he ran his hand up her thigh. The evening might yet be pleasant.

"So, how did you and Mike meet?" asked Sarah, whilst powdering their noses in the ladies' bathroom. Indigo had been waiting for this question.

"Oh, we've been friends for years. He's been really supportive. I met him when I'd just come out of a divorce." A politician's answer was all she would get.

Sarah looked surprised. She confided that she was mad about Tom, and that they'd been together on and off for years. Last year, he'd slept with an Italian woman and they'd split up, but now they were really trying to make it work. She wanted to marry him.

"Well if he mucks you about he's an idiot," said Indigo, her generous spirit fuelled by a large quantity of red wine. "You're lovely and he should appreciate you."

"Aw thanks, really? I'm so unsure of myself after our last break-up."

"Well if he doesn't treat you properly dump him, you can do better," Indigo continued. 'Listen to you giving out advice', said a small voice in the back of her head.

As Mike and Indigo walked to the taxi rank later, she chattered about the evening, holding on to his arm.

"Will you stop talking for five seconds and shut up? You're giving me earache."

Indigo reeled back in shock. She'd thought they were having a good time, and were on the same wavelength.

"Don't look at me like that." He looked uncomfortable under her hurt gaze. "I've just eaten far too much and feel a bit uncomfortable."

"Well, you did have a third helping of that chicken dish," chided Indigo, "and you ate my pudding as well as yours."

In the taxi on the way home Mike was quiet, his face a mask of bad temper. Arriving home, he headed for the whisky decanter.

"Get yourself a glass of wine." It was an order. "Sit down." He pointed to the leather sofa. Indigo sat down nervously. He stood with his back to the fireplace. "What did I say to you in the car?" He drained his glass and poured another.

"Um... I'm not sure?" Indigo started fiddling with her hair.

He swore angrily.

"I asked you not to embarrass me, didn't I? You made a fool of me. My oldest friends come to meet my girlfriend, and she spends the night flashing her legs and boobs at them..." He took another gulp.

Indigo was dumbfounded.

"What? You said my dress was ok. Appropriate."

"I share my house with you. Give you a chance, and you act like a tart and argue with me, trying to make me look stupid. Flirting and chatting them up!"

"I think you're the one who was flirting, Mike," said Indigo, her voice shaking. "What was it? 'Cor, she's nice.'"

"Well she was. Can't blame a guy for looking."

"Thanks."

"What does that mean?"

"Well, it doesn't make me feel good, does it? And then you accuse me..."

Mike's bad temper bubbling beneath the surface erupted in a climax of swearing and hysteria. Indigo stood up.

"I'm going to bed. There's no..." She screamed as his crystal glass came hurtling towards her, catching her on the cheekbone before soaking her in whisky. A thousand shiny glass fragments exploded onto the gleaming wooden floor.

"You can clean up the mess." He shoved her roughly backwards onto the sofa. "I'm sleeping in the spare room. You're an embarrassment. Don't come crawling in."

Indigo went to the downstairs toilet. There was an angry red mark on her cheekbone and a bruise already forming. Tomorrow she'd have a black eye. It stung and throbbed. Pouring herself another glass of wine, she sat on the sofa numb with shock. The jealousy, insults and put-downs had been going on for a while

11

now, and he'd shoved her a few times. Now for the first time he'd actually bruised her.

And now there was the same sick heavy feeling in her stomach that she'd experienced the night before in the dream. The tiny fleeting thought from earlier developed a voice. Mike was the dark force that pursued her. He had become something to be feared.

He said nothing about the incident the following day and Indigo was too nervous and weary to mention it. They were polite to each other and he returned to the bedroom. However, she managed to deflect his sexual advances by lying that her period had come early. In the past she had pushed his aggressive or unreasonable behaviour out of her mind, because she wanted the relationship to work. However, the mental cruelty coupled with his physical assault had damaged their relationship irreparably. His drinking and aggression was both unattractive and weak. She wished that she'd quizzed Sarah at the dinner about his past relationship with Chrissie. Why had that ended?

THREE

Final Warning

Indigo's working life was also deteriorating. Despite bringing prospective new business to the building firm, clients were slow to sign contracts for work. Jeremy Clifford-Amos was becoming increasingly stressed and bad-tempered and vented his frustration on Indigo. Unhappiness and lethargy became her new companions. She could barely be bothered to wash her hair or put on make-up in the mornings.

Three Mondays later, she crawled out of bed at 8 a.m. Complaining to Mike of stomach cramps she'd slept in one of the guest bedrooms. An empty bottle of wine lay by the side of the bed. She didn't remember drinking the entire bottle. Picking it up, she shook it and then felt the carpet by the side of the bed. The floor was dry. A DVD case lay on the floor. Ah, yes she had watched GI Jane, a film about a strong powerful woman. She had been attempting to inspire herself. Yes, that was it.

Arriving five minutes late for work, Jeremy glared at her.

"Coffee, Jeremy?"

"Yes, and one for you and bring them into the other office."

Indigo and Janey exchanged glances. The 'office of bollockings' loomed. All employees had been subjected to that on occasion.

"You are an effing powerhouse some of the time Indigo, with your good looks, little suits and ballsey attitude. But at the moment you're a mess. You ain't pulling your weight. I should fire you. You have a stain on your top. You was late this morning. You have a crap attitude. Get new clothes, pull yourself together. This is a verbal warning." Jeremy delivered this all in one breath.

Indigo began to cry. Totally drained, and being attacked on all fronts, she felt backed into a corner. Her life was a catalogue of disasters and disappointments. Jeremy was a nightmare to work for. She hated being confined to an office with him on a daily basis. He was continually screaming and ranting at the staff. He found fault constantly with her performance until her nerves were strung to snapping point. The job itself was boring and depressing. And now Mike, the man she'd put on a pedestal and thought was her life partner, had turned out to be a monster too. There was nothing like living with someone to find out what they were really like.

Her own property, that she'd told Mike she'd let out to tenants, was still empty, so that was an option. She purposely hadn't returned there even when the situation at Mike's had become difficult because she'd wanted to adjust to living with him properly. This couldn't be achieved by running back home every five minutes. It had only been a while. If she rented it out she could make an extra few hundred pounds a month but an intuition buried deep within her had stopped her.

To make matters worse, the children had both emailed her that morning to ask if she would come to Italy to meet them at their grandparents' in the summer holidays. They were going there after visiting their Dad at his house in France. They were supposed to have come to her and stay at Mike's. With awkwardness, they admitted that they weren't keen on Mike and didn't really want to stay with him. They were sorry and wanted her to be happy. Was she sure he was 'the one'? She could empathise with them fully.

Feeling miserable, she went home and began preparing dinner. Pouring herself a glass of wine, she put her iPod on the docking station and blared out Linkin Park. She had half an hour before Mike was due home from work. Placing fresh salmon on tin foil she added butter, salt and pepper, wrapped it and put it into the oven on low. New potatoes and broccoli were steaming away on the hob.

She heard the door bang. Automatically she turned down the volume.

"That's a bit loud, Babe."

"Sorry."

He came up to her and began running his hands over her body. The old magic that used to melt her body into his so that it was impossible to resist had died a dreary death. Death by abuse and tedium. He moved his hand downwards. Indigo restrained him gently.

"Dinner's cooking."

"You're been like this since you met my friends. Are you shagging one of them or both of them, 'cos you're certainly not getting it from me!" His eyes were narrow slits.

"I've had my period!"

"What, for three bloody weeks?"

He opened the oven.

"What's this? Veggie crap I suppose."

"I've done you some salmon."

"So have you still got your period?"

Indigo hesitated. She daren't lie to him.

Mike came up to her, nose to nose.

"Get upstairs," he said nastily and kissed her on the mouth.

Indigo came back downstairs an hour later crying. Her body ached as Mike had been rough with her and her wrists were bruised. The potatoes were burnt and had boiled dry and the kitchen stank. She'd never get the black off the bottom of the saucepan. The salmon was overcooked by forty-five minutes and the broccoli was a pile of green mush. Mike had gone out to the pub to play pool with his mates.

The week dragged on. Indigo could hardly bring herself to talk to Mike. He seemed unusually cheerful. Returning home from work on the Thursday, she found a note on the side. No 'phone call or text.

"Hi, Babe. Mum's a bit upset at the moment. Just fed up so going up north til Tuesday for a long weekend. Can u clean the house while I'm away? I've left u some housekeeping. See u when I get back. Love Mike. XX"

Fuming, Indigo cursed him. What a cheek! The note pretty much summed up his whole attitude towards her. He treated her either like a sex object or skivvy and frankly couldn't care less about her. This was the third trip up north he'd made in the last two months. He adored his mother but didn't normally visit her that often. It was more likely that he was going away for a dirty weekend with some woman. Despite recently turning fifty-three, he was still a womaniser.

He's too old for you anyway, whispered a small voice. Her ego could always be relied upon to make her feel better and dull the pain of rejection. This time though it had quite a mission to accomplish. Yes, they'd shared some good times together, but it had always felt as though the perfunctory dinner or drinks irritated him as all he really wanted was to get her into bed. He could be a bit of a bore too, droning on about what he wanted to do with his life, but never actually doing what he said. The main attraction had been the physical aspect as they shared pretty powerful sexual chemistry. The air sizzled between them. Indigo had been surprised when he'd asked her to move in with him. But Friday night would now be spent cleaning Mike's numerous toilets while he no doubt played away. At least she could play her music loud.

◆ ◆ ◆

"You're late!" bellowed Jeremy Clifford-Amos as Indigo hurried into the office the next morning.

Glancing at the wall clock it read three minutes past nine.

"And you're effing useless," he continued, chucking a screwed-up piece of paper at her.

He was standing in the middle of the office in his new Italian designer suit. Tall, slim and extremely bad-tempered. His bushy shoulder-length hair seemed even more puffed out that morning, and his once attractive face held an evil red glow. He'd obviously been out drinking the night before and had a hangover.

"I'm surrounded by idiots." He gestured to the site manager, quantity surveyor and handful of builders that were sitting in the office looking wary. "Get the structural engineer on the 'phone – NOW! Honeycomb walls or something. And there's some party wall issues. They've stopped the job." He stomped off to his desk glaring at her. "Now I've gotta pay these idiots for doing nothing."

Reclining in his black leather chair, he fidgeted with his Blackberry.

"And Indigo... stop sending me emails. I had seven since yesterday!"

"You told me to stop writing messages onto yellow post-it notes and to email you!" she protested. The words had sprung from her mouth before she had a chance to bite them back.

His hazel eyes went black with rage.

"How dare you speak to your chairman like that... Don't you ever answer me back!" he screamed, his face going purple. He began to rub his eyebrow back and forth, a sign that he was trying to control his temper. "You're this close to getting a written warning, Indigo!" He held his two forefingers in the air.

Suddenly he reminded her of Bobo the clown from Thomas the Tank Engine with his fuzzy hair and cross face, and she had a hysterical desire to burst out laughing. He glared back and began swearing fluently. He knew her too well.

Jeremy Clifford-Amos, ex-city trader turned self-taught building expert, was one of Indigo's ex-boyfriends. She'd met him on an Internet dating site, when she was on a long break from Mike. Jeremy, however, had turned out to be a bully, venting his rage on anyone that got on his nerves. She shuddered as a mental picture of their previous intimacy flashed through her mind.

He had been so charming when she'd first met him. They'd gone on a date to a Tudor pub in the heart of the Kent countryside. Old wooden beams, firelight and soft music surrounded them and they'd spent a wonderful evening sitting snugly together, warmed by the glow of the wood burner and their mounting lust. They watched the orange and purple hissing fire crackling and dancing in the grate, and held hands. A great deal of champagne had been drunk leaving them giggling like a couple of teenagers in love. Gazing into each other's eyes, they'd kissed with their knees touching. For Indigo it had been heaven. The evening had finished with them smoking cigarettes and tumbling into bed. Indigo hadn't smoked since university and hadn't again since that night.

"You're so pretty, Indigo," Jeremy had said, "and clever. Can't believe I'm lucky enough to be here with you. Don't ever wanna lose you. Your eyes are the same colour as your name."

After that evening they had begun to see each other regularly. He was funny, good-looking and energetic and she found that she liked him more and more. A few weeks later, his PA walked out and he offered her a job at his building firm. It was then that the relationship began to deteriorate and Indigo began to see the real man within. A month later they stopped seeing each other but he convinced her to stay on as his secretary and as she'd turned down another job to work for him, she decided to stay. Easy is not always best.

◆ ◆ ◆

Friday evening, Indigo locked the office and clip-clopped in black stilettoes and black power suit down the steep path to the car park.

"Life's too short," she muttered.

How she'd love to simply walk away from everything. The kids were happy at university and wouldn't care if she sold the family home, as long as they were all together in the holidays. She could start afresh. 'Why don't you?' The murmur at the top of her head was constant these days. In fact, mad as it seemed, she'd even begun to answer it, to argue her case. 'Leave. Be free. Live your life the way you want to, the way you need to. You're surrounded by controlling bullies.' On and on it went.

"Oh, shut up, you're giving me a headache," she snapped through gritted teeth. Indigo clattered along the pavement.

Letting herself into Mike's six-bedroom house, she glanced around at the impersonal modern decor. It was a real bachelor pad, very masculine but she'd always thought devoid of personality. There were nice pieces of furniture but nothing with any character to it. It was as if he didn't know who he was. She often felt that Mike was playing a role and wondered what the real man had once been like before this shallow, attractive and insincere man had become the mask. Indigo didn't live here at all. There was nothing of her character here. She could fill two large suitcases with her belongings.

The large open plan kitchen was a mess, with pots and pans piled in the sink. She'd left the dishes from the night before, too depressed to bother clearing up. The hob was dirty and covered in grease. The one hundred pounds he'd left on Thursday lay on the side for housekeeping.

Indigo took off her shoes and jacket, and began to clear up. Various old birthday cards stood on a shiny black marble island situated in the middle of the kitchen from months ago. 'Happy birthday son, all my love, Mum.' The second drawer down in the kitchen contained more old cards and other junk, bits of notes, etc. The temptation proved too great.

'Mike, sorry I couldn't see you on your birthday, love Katherine xxx', dated that year. Who was Katherine? she mused. He'd spent his birthday with Indigo. She remembered being surprised because he'd said he was seeing his mates but texted her on the morning of his birthday, and they'd gone to an Italian restaurant. Had his better offer cancelled, she wondered?

Flicking through old cards, she read many sent to him from a variety of women, over the years. She shouldn't have been snooping but her hand seemed to have a mind of its own. Then she saw Mike's digital camera. Recently he'd taken to holidaying alone for the odd week here and there and as Indigo zoomed through the photos this was confirmed to her. Seeing one where he'd taken a picture of himself smiling, it suddenly struck her that Mike was in fact quite a sad individual.

Suddenly amidst the mountain views and scenic lake photographs was one of a girl standing by the kitchen sink, here at his home, in her sexy underwear. 'God my bum looks big,' Indigo thought, appalled. Until it slowly, stupidly, dawned on her that her own hair was dark and the girl in the photograph's hair was light brown and that it was not Indigo's mostly naked bottom but someone else's. Zooming in she saw that that the girl was quite plain and smiling with her lips pressed together. He had taken a photograph of Indigo in exactly the same spot months before, hence her confusion. Looking at the date on the corner she saw that it had been taken at a time when she'd been seeing Mike too.

'I thought my bum wasn't that big,' she thought cattily, 'and she's plain too.'

She flicked through the rest of the photographs. The girl had taken one of him chopping onions. How romantic! Her first thought was to leave. The relationship was foul and doomed, even she knew that now. Filled with a calm, dispassionate hysteria, she wasn't sure how to react. A sickly numbness swam through her. Should she clean first and then go? The thought flitted through her mind. 'How could you even consider such a thing? He is a waking nightmare.' The small voice at the top of her skull was positively booming in an irate fashion. Indigo could imagine it belonged to a little angel who was now jumping up and down, with frustration and rage. Its halo was bobbing. 'No! You don't do his cleaning. You leave!'

19

"Alright, alright!"

Putting the money into her purse, she looked around and said again:

"Alright!"

Quietly walking around the house, she extracted every part of herself from DVDs to dirty laundry. As calculated, all her belongings fitted into two cases. Bumping them down the stairs, she stood in the hallway. Tears began to stream down her face. She caught sight of her pitiful reflection in the hall mirror looking small, sad and pale. Thanks to Mike chipping away at her self-esteem, confidence and character, she didn't know who she was anymore. Her personal identity had been torn to shreds.

"I admit defeat," she muttered, "but some battles are better lost... or are they won?"

'You've just found out what he's really like,' sang her angel, 'you've won. Only a loser would stay.'

Unfortunately, a mere mortal, Indigo was not angelic. On the contrary. The dirty pots and pans sat glumly in the sink in disarray, untouched by human hand, and the greasy hob shone in the evening sunlight. She had been cleaning the downstairs bathroom but somehow kept dropping the toilet rolls. So clumsy. They kept unravelling, one after the other, until the floors of the bathroom and hallway were covered in cheap white toilet paper.

It was a bit chilly in the house, as always, and so she turned up the heating thermostat to full blast. The house should be nice and warm for him when he returned from his weekend away, on Tuesday. Three days should be enough to get the place hot and toasty. She had unplugged the freezer too in order to use the plug socket for the hoover and had been in the middle of defrosting the fridge. Indigo was a fast worker and believed in multi-tasking. Unfortunately, she only 'remembered' this after shutting the door behind her. She wished that she could afford to stock her freezer with large quantities of haddock, salmon and steak. Maybe one day. Anyway, she'd been considerate and left Mike's keys on the side. Indigo no longer had access to his property.

Feeling vengeful, she drove to the nearest supermarket and bought two bottles of red wine and two bags of salted popcorn. One negative aspect of her life was now gone, leaving her feeling sad but lighter. It was a start.

FOUR

The Message

Returning to her own house, she found it welcoming but dusty. Despite it being July she put the heating on. Her vengeful mood gave way to fear and uncertainty halfway through the evening. She imagined Mike's fury when he discovered his lovely home a mess and boiling hot. He would be straight on the 'phone or text or even worse he might come to her house. The thought of confrontation filled her with horror. She couldn't cope with a character assassination followed by his justifications. He would win. She would be made to feel small, insignificant and worthless.

Although he was the sinner, Indigo was the one wracked with guilt due to her actions. Her ego was crushed, wounded by the image of the plain girl who was not as slim or as good looking as her. Why had he felt the need to go with another woman when he had Indigo? What was wrong with her? She poured another glass of red wine as fear gripped her, churning up bleak darkness from the pit of her stomach. To make matters worse, she had to go into the office the following morning to finish typing up an important tender for a job worth three quarters of a million pounds.

Suddenly Indigo felt too exhausted to think or worry any longer. Despite the dread of work the next day, she drained the remainder of the wine and headed for bed. Resting her head gently onto the cool white pillowcase, she closed her eyes and drifted off to sleep.

The ghost of wisdom comes in the night in the form of dreams sharing knowledge with the dreamer. The way forward is shown and choices are given. The dreamer may take control of their life, but only if they choose to...

◆ ◆ ◆

The smooth surface of the high flat mud bank was broken up by an eruption of roots from willow trees lining the river. It was a leafy place of seclusion, peace, fresh air, warmth and harmony. Shades of dark green, lime and gold flickered as the sun seared rays of brilliance through the abundance of foliage. Nature's orchestra strummed an accompaniment to the bubbling, gurgling force of the river that rushed in two directions past the small island.

A trodden pathway wove through the trees leading to a flat wooden plank that formed a footbridge over the water. On the island by the footbridge sat a group of people clothed in thin white linen gowns. A long-haired man stood at the centre of the group. He had knowledge of each person's life purpose in an old cloth cap that he held in his hand. He randomly selected old pieces of parchment from within the cap. Walking to each person, he touched them upon their shoulder, and informed them what their life purpose was to be.

Pulling out a slip of paper, he walked to a girl with golden hair: "Entertainer. You will give happiness and help others in this way."

Taking another note, he read out: "Spiritual healer." Walking around the back of the group, he touched the shoulder of the girl with long dark hair. Her eyes widened and she reeled backwards with shock. The girl was Indigo.

"It is your gift from God, to attempt to alleviate the suffering of others," he explained. "One has to draw upon strength, wisdom and shared knowledge in order to empower others: healer and peacemaker."

Indigo awoke, blinking into the semi-darkness. A deep feeling of warmth and peace filled her entire body.

◆ ◆ ◆

"Did you `phone Derek Jones, yesterday?" Jeremy banged the white board nailed to the wall with his fist. The board contained written lists of potential clients and current jobs. "I asked you to chase them up. They must have made a decision by now. What takes so long? I need to know!" Raising his voice, Jeremy loomed over her, frowning. Dressed in ripped jeans and a black sweater he stood with his hands resting on his narrow hips.

"Yes. I `phoned them, but they weren't in and so I left a message."

"Saying what?"

"Just checking that they'd received the estimate," Indigo lied.

She'd `phoned them earlier in the week, but knew that people hated being hounded. The prospective client needed time to make a decision about who was going to do their building works. Yes, a follow-up call was good but not constant calls every day which was what Jeremy wanted her to do.

He glanced at his watch.

"`Phone them again. Tell them we need to get the work booked in. I'm going shooting. Have you nearly finished? I want that posted by lunchtime. Recorded delivery and make sure you get a receipt. I'll know if you haven't, Indigo." His hazel eyes narrowed. "I'm watching you! Make sure you lock the filing cabinets and the office."

"Ok."

"Yes Chairman!'"

"Yes Chairman." Indigo looked down at the site manager's notes.

"Indigo, you've got a bad attitude and you're a mess!" He stood by the door pointing at her, and then left.

Tears threatened as she sat in the office alone. She couldn't deal with all this conflict in her life. She didn't invite it. She was a calm, decent, loving person yet her boyfriend and employer were both hideous people. Mike was cruel, dishonest and treated her like a piece of shit. Indigo knew that she could never see him again and she was dreading the consequence of her impulsive actions. He really frightened her. Jeremy Clifford-Amos was a bully, and of similar character to Mike. Her life had become untenable and depressing. She couldn't bear it. If it wasn't for the children, would she carry on with her life? What was the point of her anyway? As she sank into the negative swamp of self-pity it sucked her down further, willing her to drown, to succumb to dark forces. Indigo loathed self-pity but here it was in the guise of warped comfort.

The peace brought to her during the night made her realise the extent of the discord in her life. The man with the long hair and blue eyes had been surrounded by a white shimmering aura that exuded love and peace. Indigo didn't want darkness and stress in her life. She wanted the light, hungered for it. The very thought of a different type of existence pulled her temporarily from the swamp.

An email popped up from the Canterbury Chamber of Commerce. Indigo was about to delete it without reading it, but for some reason she opened it instead.

'Reiki 1: Spiritual Guided Energy: Are you feeling stressed, confidence need boosting...?' Butterflies tore through her stomach. 'Spiritual Healer' had been the purpose given to her by the man in her dream, and now this email. Nervously, she clicked onto the link.

'You can learn Reiki to treat yourself and, later, others. This course will teach you the foundations of Reiki: the history, its ideals and principles. We will approach the energy systems relating to our chakras, the hand positions for self-treatment and much more...'

What did this mean? A slit of brilliant white light flashed for a fraction of a second in her subconscious. But it was enough. Indigo reached for her mobile and dialled the number of the Canterbury Reiki Centre. The call went to voicemail. She hesitated and then blurted out a message:

"I saw your Reiki advertisement from the Chamber of Commerce. I'm... I need some help. I don't know what to do..." Her voice broke. "Indigo Summers. You'll have my number on your `phone. Thanks, bye."

Tears splashed onto the site manager's notes melting the ink and blurring the text. Like a rainstorm that began gradually the tears were soon torrential. Aggressively shoving the contents of the desk onto the floor, she banged her head onto the desk and sobbed. The office `phone rang and was left unanswered. Indigo took out her compact mirror. She looked vile, black tears from her mascara had left streaks down her tired old face. Her eyes were bloodshot and red. She looked like a demon. Cleaning up her face with a make-up wipe, she tried to dry her eyelashes with a tissue. Re-applying make-up, she blew her nose. Jeremy Clifford-Amos was right about one thing, she was a mess.

Checking her online banking she saw that her wages had gone in the day before. She looked around the office and decided that it was time to leave and slowly put all her personal belongings into a carrier bag. Going through her drawers, she took out note books, adding some envelopes and a packet of paper. Indigo wiped her nose dolefully on her sleeve.

Her mobile `phone rang.

"Hi, Indigo. My name is Rebecca, from the Canterbury Reiki Centre."

"Oh yes, hi. Thanks for getting back to me." She felt so weak she could barely be bothered to speak. It was as though she was being strangled. That must be where the saying 'all choked up' came from. Rebecca seemed to realise this and kept it calm and brief.

"Have you experienced Reiki before?"

"No. But I'm in such a mess - my work, I hate it, my boss is a bully. My personal life's a joke. I'm just so completely exhausted."

"I have a cancellation tomorrow morning, if you'd like to come along. We can just chat or you may find a session of Reiki beneficial."

"Thanks, ok. That's great! Yes, I'd like to try it." Indigo sniffed. There was something in Rebecca's voice that gave her a sense of hope.

After the telephone conversation she felt the same calm responsiveness she'd experienced after the spiritual healer dream. Rational thought returned with a feeling of serenity. Picking up a white envelope she addressed it to Jeremy Clifford-Amos and then wrote a quick note:

'Jeremy, can't work for you anymore. You're a bully. Here are the keys to the office. Indigo.'

Checking the office thoroughly, she headed for the door. Locking it behind her, Indigo placed the keys into the envelope, sealed it and posted them into the red post box on the corner of the street. For the second time in two days she closed the door on a negative part of her life. There was no turning back on either. The question was: where would she go from here?

Indigo slept badly that night. Her equilibrium was shot to pieces by the events of the week and she felt fretful, lonely and anxious. Her sleep was peppered by strange dreams.

◆ ◆ ◆

Indigo entered an ancient church. A large oak crucifix hung high up upon the wall behind the white altar. The priest was preaching his sermon but she couldn't hear what he was saying. The sun streamed through the stained glass windows in penetrating beams, projecting colourful images onto the pews and worshippers below. She moved like a ghost amongst the people. They had no identity and she was invisible to them. The preacher walked from the pulpit up a narrow, steep staircase whilst delivering his sermon. He stepped onto glass beams that held the roof in place, up above the congregation. It was as if he was walking on colourful air. His long robes swished on the smooth surface. The place was light, serene and full of love.

Indigo awoke with a start and drank some water before returning to sleep.

◆ ◆ ◆

In the second dream of the night, she is wandering in an old 17th century mansion. The house appears to be empty and the floor consists of cold grey flag stones. Turning to her right she notices some stone stairs leading down into the basement. Hesitating, she feels fearful, but curious, and ventures downstairs into a dim passage strewn with leaves, mud and other natural debris. Cobwebs glued to the ceiling wave tendrils in a thin breeze blowing through a crack in a shabby wooden door. Tentatively she peeps through the gap. Beyond is a murky corridor that bends to the right. Heading through the door she follows the stone path.

Opening a further door she moves into a plush interior. The room to the inner basement is palatial, boasting expensive antique French furniture of many shades of red with curling, swirling gold patterns and borders. Huge canvasses of exquisite oil paintings: landscapes and seascapes and faceless portraits look down from the walls. Rich colourful tapestries hang from other walls. Thick red rugs cover the floor. A second room is filled with cream and peach silk that adorns the walls, ceiling and floors. A large bed is covered in bedding of the same colour. There are further rooms of the same kind but she can't see them. There is an impression of freedom and space, a quality to the place that she cannot comprehend. A secret haven, it possesses the richness and privacy of the soul.

Indigo's eyes open. She understands that she is looking at her own soul. Sleep overcomes her once more.

◆ ◆ ◆

The preacher returned. This time she could hear his calm voice, devoid of accent.

'The passage is representative of the physical body that encompasses the soul. The brain barricades and protects you from harm, but the subconscious will deliver. Dreams impart knowledge, insight. The soul shines through the eyes but can turn inwards seeing into the spiritual self, into the being within. The soul is the energy source that fuels the self through life, igniting flames of passion. The soul is the life force. We are spiritual beings living in physical bodies, not physical beings with a spiritual side.'

The preacher turned and looked at Indigo. His eyes were a piercing bright blue and full of strength, love and hypnotic light.

◆ ◆ ◆

Indigo awoke gasping into the darkness. The message was clear. Take notice and act immediately or face dire consequences. Her time had come. The higher powers had run out of patience.

FIVE

The Journey Begins

She awoke at seven feeling dreadful and lay staring at the vast print of the North Berwick coastline that covered one wall. The photograph had been taken about ten years ago, in the days when she had allowed her creative aspect to flourish. The appointment at the Canterbury Reiki Centre was at ten. Indigo didn't want to go. She wanted to cancel. She wasn't in the mood. But the alternative was to lie in bed with negative thoughts tormenting her and so she clambered out of bed grimacing at her pale, worn reflection.

"What an old bag... I used to be so pretty!"

Indigo shuffled into the kitchen muttering 'tea and lots of it'. By the third cup, the decision was made to have a bath and reluctantly go to the appointment, although she had already concluded that it was a load of nonsense and wouldn't work. Images from the vivid dreams came to mind, but she shoved them away. Every negative thought in the vicinity came to the party in her skull that morning. Gleefully they crammed their way into her brain, chattering all the way to the Centre. By the time she arrived, Indigo felt suffocated by bad temper and exhaustion.

The Reiki Centre was situated down a lane near Canterbury High Street. Turning into the car park, she sat in the car for a few moments trying to summon the energy and inclination to go in. Her state of irritability was so intense that she actually felt uncomfortable in her own skin. It was as though she was knotted up and overheated inside. The urge to drive away was huge, but she reasoned that she would still be charged if she didn't go in, and she couldn't afford to pay money for nothing. A tiny positive voice in her mind, almost crushed by the negative party-goers, squeaked that maybe this would be good for her. New experiences were vital or she'd never get out of her tedious rut. Grimly, at exactly 10 a.m. Indigo got out of the car and walked to the white building.

Entering the Centre, an overwhelming sense of peace and calm engulfed her. There was no-one in Reception. The room was simple and comfortable, containing plants, a white sofa and a coffee table. On the wall were leaflets of the classes the Centre ran: yoga, Reiki, past life regression and karate. Indigo sank down onto the sofa. A subtle odour of lavender drifted to her nostrils and the dulcet tones of a meditation track hummed in the background.

The treatment rooms appeared to be hidden away behind a large wooden door. Shutting her gritty, tired eyes she rested her head back, soaking up the unusual atmosphere that swirled around her. The fingers of tension and irritability were slowly being prized from her bones. Just as they were about to let go one by one, a noise beyond the door brought her back to reality. The fingers snapped shut and her eyelids flicked open.

A woman stood by the connecting door. She was tall and attractive, dressed in a purple t-shirt and black trousers. She exuded strength but it was the intense look in her eyes that caught Indigo's attention. As their eyes met she felt a strong sense of familiarity and connection. It was bizarre.

"Hi, I'm Rebecca." She walked towards her. Indigo rose and gripped her hand.

"Indigo, pleased to meet you, and thanks for fitting me in at such short notice." She gestured to the sofa, "So comfortable. Knocked me out."

"It's the Reiki," she smiled. "You can feel the energy. It's everywhere in the building."

Indigo stood awkwardly, feeling uptight and adolescent next to the calm being by her side. Rebecca handed her a clip-board and a pen.

"If you could just fill out the details... I have a few preparations to make and then I'll be back." She disappeared through the mysterious door.

Indigo made steps along a new pathway that day. As she travelled along the narrow corridor to the treatment room later, towards an experience that she'd never encountered before, she had no way of knowing that it was about to change her entire life.

The room was lit by candles. A small desk sat in one corner. The treatment table for the client dominated the floor. There was a small seating area at the back of the room with bottled water and magazines. Indigo could feel a strong energy in the room. It made her feel relaxed, almost sleepy. The scent of lavender oil was apparent. Soft melodious tones of Reiki healing music with soft pipes floated about the room.

They sat for a moment in the seating area and Indigo told her about recent events. It came out in a big gush and tears welled up in her eyes. Rebecca sat and listened to her crying, ranting and occasionally swearing. It was as if her eyes could see into one's very soul.

"I'm a bit scared about this... Reiki," Indigo blurted. "Nothing awful will happen will it? I won't have spirits come to me or anything? I don't like that sort of thing. Freaks me out."

"Reiki is a healing energy that comes from a place of love. Only good can come to you. I am a channel for the Reiki energy. It comes from a higher source. You are safe."

Still terrified, Indigo climbed onto the white softness of the Reiki treatment table and Rebecca covered her with a thin blanket. Lying tense, like a ramrod, she listened to her murmuring reassurance and tried to have faith.

Standing behind her, Rebecca placed her hands under Indigo's lower skull. She shut her eyes, expecting to feel nothing. Suddenly waves and waves of sensation began to flow through her, powerful, warm and flooding. Purples swam through her mind changing to dark indigo, greens and blues. Blankets of colour engulfed her. Then she felt a powerful force, a heat on her face like dragon's breath and a strong scent of lavender. Her head felt lighter. The comforting heat moved to her ears. As it travelled to her throat, Indigo felt choked for a moment. A heaviness pressing down onto her chest, and panic encompassed her. She thought she was having a heart attack.

"What's that?" Indigo muttered, twitching.

"Just the Reiki pressing down."

The Reiki overpowered the panic and Indigo relaxed. A prickly chill filled her body moving up and down. Suddenly, she felt frozen from the neck downwards, but pressed down by a force onto the bed. A soothing heat wrapped itself around her feet and ankles, and warm waves began to glide through her body once more.

Rebecca returned to her head area, and the colours began again: red, lilac, blue and yellow. Now completely relaxed, Indigo surrendered to the energy. Then Rebecca moved away. Indigo felt disappointed. She wanted to lie there forever absorbing the delicious sensations of warmth and power. A small bell sounded in the distance. For a moment she lay there pinned down and then gradually moved to a sitting position. It was as though she was shaking off a covering of heavy blankets. Indigo felt completely disorientated, a bit light-headed but on a massive high.

"Are you ok?"

"That was amazing!" Indigo told her how the Reiki had affected her.

"You're vibrating on a very high frequency," Rebecca said, "that's why you feel the Reiki so strongly."

"Really?"

"Yes, your chakras were completely blocked and the energy wasn't flowing. It's not surprising that you have felt so tired. All the negative aspects in your life are causing you to leak energy. When we have a lot of negativity, it stops the flow of energy. I will give you some exercises to ground and protect yourself."

Indigo swung her legs off the bed. She felt featherweight, vibrant and bouncing with energy. Her mind was clear, maybe for the first time ever. As she walked to the seated area, she began to shake her leg. It was as though something was pulling at it.

"You must drink lots of water, and if you feel a little different, don't worry, that's normal. You have had a massive shift occur within you."

Indigo made another appointment for two weeks time and left. Driving home she sang at the top of her voice to the radio. Images of the campervan owned by her friend Charlotte kept coming into her mind. During their last conversation Charlotte had tried to convince her to take it.

"Have the campervan, Indigo. I don't need it anymore."

Charlotte had married well. She lived with her husband in a seven-bedroom house in Canterbury. They also owned two holiday homes in Italy and France. Her husband Thomas worked as a surgeon at Kent and Canterbury hospital.

"Or if you're too proud to accept it as a gift, then borrow it indefinitely."

Indigo had been reluctant to accept her offer due to her relationship with Mike and her job. She hadn't wanted to go anywhere. Now she couldn't wait to leave. She called her friend the moment she got home. There was no time to waste. Charlotte was delighted.

"What made you change your mind? You sound great. I was so worried about you!"

"I'll email you in a couple of days," Indigo said. "Tell you all about it then... in a bit of a rush. Charlotte, thanks!"

"Oh, I'm intrigued!"

Next she emailed the children and told them that she was going away for a couple of weeks for a short break. Then she called her mobile `phone provider and asked to change her number. Indigo had been going to take the fallout on the chin, for wrecking Mike's house and leaving Jeremy and her job without notice. Temporarily deluded, she had been filled with remorse, thinking that she had to take what was coming to her; but after today, she questioned why she should put up with any more unpleasantness from either of them.

She had been a good partner to Mike, considerate and loving. She had put up with bullying and abuse from Jeremy and had worked hard for him too. She didn't deserve what they had given to her in return. Indigo was too good for them. Today she drew a line under it all. It was time to move on.

"Your number will be changed in two hours!" said the mobile `phone operator. "Is there anything else I can do for your today, Ms Summers?"

"Two hours! Brilliant." Indigo couldn't believe how simple it had been. "No, that's great, thanks."

Next she dragged a dusty old atlas out from under the bookcase. Opening it with her eyes shut, she placed her finger on a spot.

"This is where I will go," she concluded dramatically, hoping that it wasn't the middle of the sea or, worse, just down the road from where she was now. Her finger landed on the east coast of Scotland. She looked further with her eyes screwed up: North Berwick. How odd. Indigo knew North Berwick. Not well, but she'd been there ten years ago, after visiting family in Edinburgh. Hence the huge photo print on her bedroom wall.

"Ok! North Berwick it is." Looking around her bedroom she pulled down her suitcase and began to pack.

Indigo left Canterbury at 3 a.m. to avoid the traffic on the M25. After that it was straight up the M1. Adventure and the open road lay in front of her... her journey into the unknown had begun.

SIX

Across the Border

Indigo could see the blue and white Scottish saltire waving in the distance at 11 o'clock. The vast North Sea lay sprawled out to the right, glinting sapphire blue in the sunlight. White puffy clouds floated like air boats amidst the azure sky. Slowing down the campervan, she opened the window and took in the view. Dark cliffs graduated down to the ocean, littered with shrubs and rogue trees. An array of bright orange poppies, yellow buttercups and daisies grew from the wild grasses at the side of the road, including some tall blue and lilac flowers that waved back and forth in the breeze. A waft of fresh air laced with sea salt filled the interior of the van. Seagulls squawked in the distance. Leaving England, she crossed the border into Scotland. She had arrived. Suddenly she felt safe.

She stopped in Haddington, a small historic town situated off the motorway to buy supplies and freshen up. She felt exhausted physically, mentally, emotionally and spiritually. But amidst the gloom there was a weak flame burning, and every positive act and thought she had fuelled it. In time it would blaze like an inferno. But the journey had just begun. There was a remote place she remembered, in North Berwick along the seafront, where she could park the campervan. She would spend the night alongside the ocean soaking up the natural world. The healing could then begin.

Parking the van by the cliffs, she got out and stretched. It was very windy, but the campervan was partially protected by the cliff face to her right. North Berwick sat to the left along the coast, like a picture postcard. Rows of colourful houses, green, yellow and pink, sat in proud rows overlooking the huge rolling breakers that raced up the golden sand. The Seabird Centre perched up on the rocks cut into the sea in the distance. Indigo remembered the fast boat trip that she and the children had taken out to the Bass Rock, a mass of volcanic rock that protruded out of the water. She couldn't see it from where she had parked because the rock face jutted out into the ocean. But it was there, disappearing on occasion like a magician when the mist came in from the sea.

Putting the shopping away in the small cupboards that lined part of one wall, Indigo looked out of the window. For a moment she felt a flicker within of the thick ache that had filled her since her discovery about Mike and leaving her job. Reiki had helped immensely but the wounds were so raw, too new to heal completely with one session. The sea will help, she thought. Making her bed at the far end of the campervan, she mused that she was fortunate to have the opportunity to dump her problems and move on, if only for a short while. The campervan was modern inside with a fitted kitchen, running water, a narrow shower and toilet, dining and bedroom area. It looked like an ambulance from the outside without the markings. There was a water tank at the top that caught rain water. A small generator ran the electricity. Indigo had brought candles and lanterns for lighting.

Taking a sandwich and beaker of wine, she locked the van and walked down a couple of steps of rough slate to the beach below. Despite it being July, the wind held a chill and she had added a quilted jacket, woollen hat that covered her ears and wellingtons with thick socks. Walking towards the cliffs she squelched and crunched her way through rock pools adorned with thousands of small seashells of ruby, emerald, silver and cream. The sea's treasure chests were full of jewels. The tide had turned and was coming in rapidly, tearing up the beach at speed, great frothing tips flinging debris and seaweed onto the beach.

Indigo walked towards a cluster of rocks that formed a seat. Placing a towel onto the rocks she sat down and gazed out to sea, sipping wine and breathing in the air. She had escaped from tedium, from the continual mind games, from the pain, from being tormented on a daily basis. By her second cupful, exhaustion reigned and she began to cry. The events of the past months had ripped her apart, and now finally she let her emotions go. She cried silently.

Streaks of gold penetrated the grey gloom of the last light. The jagged ebony cliffs loomed, stretching their razor sharp limbs outwards cutting a pathway into the ocean. Harsh darkness contrasted with the light reflected upon the water. The even mechanism of the waves disrupted by inky crags churned the smooth water into a rage of white foam. Seated within the rugged folds of the cliffs, Indigo pondered life. The scene before her was timeless. A natural beauty neither created nor sculpted by man. It told no tales of history, or pain, or sadness. The passing years had left no apparent scars on nature; but as she sat there she began to reflect upon her own scars. The choices she had made and the consequences suffered due to those choices. The powerful scent of salt and seaweed fused with the roar of the tide pounding upon the headland. The seagulls screamed in shrill unison and the wind in flight howled hysterically around the cliffs, evoking nostalgia within Indigo for safer and happier times.

A distant figure appeared splashing through the waves as if he had run straight out of the ocean. He had been jogging around the cliffs from bay to bay. This was a dangerous pastime unless the runner had a good knowledge of the tides. The North Sea could be ruthless and when the tide turned it came in swiftly washing away anything in its path. The runner appeared to be heading towards her but she was hidden within the darkness of the rocks. The moonlight illuminated a long strip of surface water that ran from the ocean up to the high tide mark on the beach. He ran past her, his feet leaving deep footprints in the sand that vanished as if by magic. She couldn't see his face but the stature told her that he was tall and strong.

Droplets of rain hit her wellingtons and waterproof jacket. The pattering increased and Indigo looked up at the sky. Pulling off her hat she let the water stream over her face soaking her hair. She had been sitting there for hours and dusk had long since closed the day. Shivering, she realised that she was frozen. Returning to the campervan, she removed her wet clothes and put them on the drier. Lighting a lantern, she climbed into bed snuggling under the thick soft duvet.

◆ ◆ ◆

Indigo writhed on the bed. Beads of sweat began to form on her body. She was wandering through barren wasteland. The sky was dark and sinister with racing black clouds. The air and earth felt rough and dry. She was lost, ambling aimlessly, not knowing which direction would take her home. Suddenly she felt herself being pushed by a force to the edge of the land that ended abruptly giving way to a slope of black rock. At the bottom of the slope was a volcanic crater filled with scarlet fire that bubbled and popped. Outside of the crater, miles below, lay the sea dark and still. Suddenly her world tilted and she fell, rolling down the hill at speed. Desperately she tried to claw hold of something to break her fall but the slope was like marble. She screamed in terror, a hoarse animalistic sound. She was about to burn to death. A brilliant white force picked her up and tossed her somersaulting through the air. Terror consumed her. She landed on her feet in a graveyard in front of a white tombstone. The ground around it was bare. The engraving on the stone said 'Indigo Summers' and her birthdate, but she couldn't see the date of her death.

◆ ◆ ◆

She awoke with a start, bathed in cold sweat although her body was burning hot. Her heart was beating at an explosive pace, and she could barely catch her breath. Disorientated, it took her a moment before she realised that she was in the campervan, it was late at night and someone was outside banging on the door.

A surge of dread and fear shot through her. Instinctively, she pulled the duvet up to her chin. If she kept quiet she could pretend that there was no-one in the van. But after screaming like a banshee, she doubted whoever it was would believe that. Illogically she wondered what would happen to her if they stole the campervan with her in the back of it. In her delirious state it didn't occur to her that thieves wouldn't knock first. Her heart was still hammering at top speed inside her chest. Her head felt muzzy and feverish.

A voice now accompanied the banging. It was male, Scottish and irate.

"This is Lothian and Borders Police. If you don't open the door I will force entry."

Relieved, Indigo opened the window and winced as the policeman shone his powerful torch into her eyes.

"I had a nightmare," she croaked. Her throat felt sore.

"This is not a campsite. You'll have to move on," he said crossly. "Are you alone? What was all the screaming about?"

"Nightmare. Yes, I'm alone."

As if she was going to drive around looking for a campsite in the middle of the night. She was beginning to feel odd. She didn't feel well at all, and the policeman's attitude was getting on her nerves.

"Do you have any identification?" she asked huskily, rubbing her throat. Her glands were up on one side.

He held up his badge and shone the torch on it.

"PC MacLeod, Lothian and Borders Police, based in North Berwick," he said curtly.

"Give me a minute, and could you turn your torch off? You're blinding me."

As she scrambled about feeling for her white fluffy dressing gown, she could hear him grumbling to himself outside, something about 'mad English' and how little he was paid. Clambering off the bed, blood rushed to her head and she toppled over crashing to the floor. The policeman banged on the door.

"What's going on?"

"Not feeling good."

"Can you open the door, or do I have to get a wrench out of the boot?"

"I'll try," she called feebly.

Pulling herself up by the work surface, she stumbled to the door and opened it. The policeman entered immediately, and demanded to know where the light switch was. Flicking it on, the interior was filled with light.

Indigo found herself looking at a tall good-looking man of around forty, with piercing green eyes and stubble. He was slim, fit and bad tempered. He narrowed his eyes taking in her appearance. Her indigo eyes were huge in her pale face and her dark brown hair was tousled. She felt lightheaded, as though she wasn't really there. Perhaps she was still asleep.

"Is this real?" she murmured.

"Have you been using drugs or alcohol?" He whipped a note book out of his back pocket. "Is this your campervan?"

"No, I decided to go away for the weekend and so I nicked one from the showroom down the road," she said crossly, glaring at him.

"Really?" He didn't find this funny. "Perhaps I should arrest you then."

Beads of sweat began to trickle down her face, and she swayed. Sinking down onto the bed, she lay down.

"What do you think you're doing?" he said. "Don't you think I've got better things to do with my time?"

"Have you? Look I'm sorry, but I've had a rough couple of weeks and I'm just really run down and feeling awful. I think I've caught a cold or something. Truly." She pointed to her handbag on the floor. "Driving licence and proof of ownership of the van are in there and the van belongs to my friend Charlotte Rhys-Davis. Her number's on my `phone." Indigo began to cry. Her body was devoid of energy and she felt like a ragdoll; she couldn't even raise her head.

The policeman picked up her bag and went through her documents, writing down some numbers from her `phone.

"You'd better get back to bed then. I'll put in my report that you've become unwell and are unable to move the vehicle at this time."

Indigo began to shiver and he looked bewildered for a moment.

"Do you have any paracetamol?" he asked.

"No, nothing."

"Plenty of wine, I see, but no paracetamol. Tourists! I'll see if I have some in the car. You'd better take a couple, I don't want you dying on my watch. Far too much paperwork."

Indigo felt too ill to reply. He came back with a box of pills and handed her two with a bottle of water from the kitchen. Opening the side cupboard he took out a couple of blankets and covered her over.

"Not in my job description. But there you go."

Indigo closed her aching eyes.

"You can't leave the van unlocked." He picked up her keys from the table. "I'll lock the door and post them in the window." His voice was distant, miles away. "You'll have moved on by the time I come back on shift tomorrow?"

Indigo had fallen asleep, and awoke late the next day to the sound of the sea crashing onto the beach and the rain hammering onto the roof of the van. For a moment she lay there feeling cosy and warm enjoying the sound of the ocean. Suddenly, she sneezed violently and sat up. Her head still felt a bit heavy, but her sore throat had gone. Her nose was running though. She had developed a summer cold. Blankets covered her, and suddenly memories of the cross policeman entered her consciousness and she groaned.

There was no way she could drive in this state. She felt exceptionally weak and a little dizzy. Perhaps the policeman wouldn't come back after all and she could stay a bit longer. He'd probably gone home to his wife and kids and forgotten all about her. To be honest, at that precise moment in time, she felt too ill to care.

She managed to get to the bathroom, and returned to bed with a toilet roll, and her mobile `phone. Sneezing, she emailed Rebecca at the Canterbury Reiki Centre and told her that she was feeling ill, tearful and weak and about the awful dream. Curling up she fell asleep. She must have slept all afternoon, because she was awoken around 5 p.m. by a rap at the door.

"Who is it?" she called.

"PC MacLeod, may I come in?"

His tone was level and friendlier than the night before.

"It's open," she called.

He popped his head around the door.

"You're in bed. I saw the van still here and thought that you were either stoned out of your head or genuinely ill."

On cue, Indigo sneezed five times in a row. She waved him in.

"Come in, if you want to risk catching my germs."

He grinned and walked in, closing the door behind him. He removed his police cap. He was really handsome, film star quality.

"I gave you a bit of a hard time last night. I meet some real scum in this job sometimes, and to be honest I thought you were on drugs to begin with."

"Only the paracetamol you gave me."

"Have you had any today?"

Indigo shook her head.

"I just about summoned the energy to make it to the bathroom."

"You've not had anything to eat or drink?"

"Water. I've slept most of the day. I felt a bit dizzy earlier and weak, not up to driving."

"You'll be ok for a few days here." He filled the kettle. "I'm not a Mr Darcy type, so don't think I am. I just know how shit it is to feel awful when you're on your own."

"I'm Indigo, by the way."

"PC MacLeod." He handed her two paracetamol out of the packet.

"Don't you have a Christian name?"

"Is it appropriate? I am on duty."

"We're only having a cup of tea together. Aren't we?"

There was one cup on the work surface. PC MacLeod added another.

"Don't mind if I do. I do community police work so I suppose this comes under that heading." He handed her a cup of tea and a couple of digestive biscuits. "My name is William, after William Wallace."

"Suits you." Indigo took a sip of tea. "Nice cup of tea, officer."

"I tell you my name, something I never do to a member of the public, and then you call me 'officer'. And surprised you've heard of William Wallace, English." He smiled.

"My parents are Scottish."

"Ah, so you just sound English then..."

Her mobile 'phone flashed. The email was from Rebecca.

'Hi, Indigo. You've been through a great deal. Don't worry, you are clearing out all old negative aspects of your life. It is quite normal to feel like this. The dream is representative of your old life, urging you to make changes. We all have a limited time to live. If you embrace your spiritual side then the quality of your life will improve. If you need to talk to me about anything, please contact me. Blessings, Rebecca.'

"So did you just fancy a holiday then?" said William. He sat down at the end of the bed.

"Kind of." Indigo fidgeted with her tea cup. She was suddenly aware that she must look a real mess having not long woken up. The paracetamol were beginning to work and she was feeling better. He sat there in silence watching her.

"Things have been a bit difficult lately in England and I had to get away."

"You mentioned this last night."

"I don't want to bore you with it."

"You won't. But only tell me if you want to."

Indigo took a deep breath, and begun with the situation with Mike, leaving out the violence and Jeremy Clifford-Amos. William sat there drinking his tea. He raised his eyebrows a few times when she explained how the men in her life had behaved towards her and smiled when she mentioned the Reiki.

"I think getting away to clear your head was wise," he said simply. "The Scottish air will set you straight."

"I'm thinking of renting out the house and moving up for a while. Maybe get a room somewhere," she found herself saying. "My children are at Leeds University which is roughly half-way, and my family are from here. I need a change."

He nodded.

"Change is good."

Indigo was about to ask him about himself, when his radio crackled. He stepped outside and she could hear him talking.

"I've got to go... accident." He put his cap back on. "Thanks for the tea. Lock the door." He left without looking at her. Switching the siren on, he zoomed off at top speed.

Indigo fished her hand mirror out of her hand bag. She looked fresh and natural, but a lump of black sleep from old mascara sat in the corner of her right eye and there was a smudge of dirt on the end of her nose.

SEVEN

Moving Up

Indigo slept well that night and awoke feeling refreshed and hungry. She took a shower and washed her hair. Putting on some make-up, jeans and a t-shirt, she felt almost normal. Glancing at her reflection in the mirror she thought that she looked less stressed and worn.

After a breakfast of vegetarian bacon, eggs and three cups of tea she decided to go for a walk along the beach. Hauling on her wellingtons she jumped down onto the sand. The sky was deep blue and the sea twinkled as if a million diamonds were balancing on the tips of the waves. The air was pure and laced with the scent of the seaweed littering the sand. Clambering over light grey slate, she examined the numerous rock pools. A perfectly sculptured green crab with big pincers lay amongst the sea shells. It looked like a child's plastic toy.

Paddling in the low tide she saw a jellyfish being carried on the waves. It resembled an ornate bowl. There were a number of them washed up on the sand. Indigo took a photograph of one with her mobile `phone. It was a bit like an eyeball, shiny with a purple iris and dark centre. She poked it with her foot. Suddenly a golden Labrador came running up to her, a young dog and full of fun. He nosed the jellyfish, smearing it over the sand. Survival was tough even for a jellyfish.

Indigo climbed over dark rocks covered with khaki green vegetation. The seaweed strands were long with rows of bubbles attached. She walked over them carefully as they were slippery, enjoying the popping sound they made under her weight.

Eventually she reached the Seabird Centre. By this time the beach was filling up with families and young children. The children were building sandcastles and wading up to their waists in the cold ocean. Sitting on the balcony of the Seabird Centre's coffee shop, she felt totally relaxed, sipping rich frothy cappuccino and enjoying the view.

The sea lapped against the harbour wall and stretched out to the horizon. Deep, dark, mysterious Prussian blue glinted in the sunlight. Blue gave way to emerald as the water became shallow and black where rocks secretly hid just beneath the surface. The cerulean sky was clear of clouds and a mild breeze blew tendrils of her long dark hair onto her face sticking to her lipstick. It was a hot summer day and even the breakers that usually tore up the beach gathering speed and height were lethargic and sluggish. The sand was warm and golden.

The Bass Rock poked out of the sea in the distance, like a giant's head boasting a thick head of white hair; a haven for nesting seagulls, puffins, gannets and rare birds. The whiteness was in fact a covering of bird excrement, nesting seabirds and their eggs. A small lighthouse sat on a ledge to the right of the rock and an old derelict fortress clung to the left side of the island. The outer walls were still intact despite being pounded by giant dark winter waves. Some of the structure had crumbled but most of the battlements remained intact.

Her mobile `phone rang. It was Charlotte.

"Hi, how are things?"

Indigo told her what had occurred since her arrival, and then added cautiously: "Charlotte, I need a change. I'll miss you, but I need to do something else for a while."

"What were you thinking?"

Indigo took a deep breath.

"I'm gonna move up here. I need to..." she paused, "...recover. Not just from Mike and Clifford-Amos, but from the divorce... everything. I know I've been divorced for a while and I'm over all that crap, but I need a fresh start."

"Yeah. I see that. I'm not surprised actually. I'll miss you of course, but I can fly up and visit. Scotland's not far and it's not as if we can't afford it."

"The only thing is the house. I don't really want to sell it. It's security and there's quite a lot of equity in it, about a hundred grand, but I'm not sure I can rent it out in the state it's in."

"What's wrong with it? Your house is really homely, and the garden's big."

"The kitchen's shabby and dated."

"I'm having a thought," said Charlotte. "Let me make a few calls. I have one of my solutions brewing! Indigo, you are sure, yeah?"

"One hundred per cent."

"Leave it with me..."

"Charlotte, what are you thinking?"

"I'll call you in a bit. You know I like to be useful."

Indigo smiled. Charlotte was a good friend and enjoyed nothing better that fixing and arranging. In her current state, Indigo welcomed any positive intervention.

Walking back along the beach, she watched the yachts sailing at speed. The lifeboat was also out, on a practice drill. The North Sea was beautiful but could be deadly. For a moment Mike's face loomed into her thoughts, and she shuddered as a dull thud hit her stomach. The nightmare had been poignant. For too long she had wandered alone without direction, in a state of emotional turmoil, the victim of others battling with their own issues. After a twenty minute walk she arrived back at the campervan. Her mobile rang. It was Charlotte.

"I have a solution. You remember my friend Sandra?"

"Yeah, tall, blonde."

"Yes. Well, her son and his fiancée are expecting a baby. They're twenty, and he's just been made redundant. They need a place of their own. A home with a garden. She's already got a two-year old and they're living with her mother."

"Ok...?"

"They're on the housing association waiting list but there are hardly any decent properties going in Canterbury. I mean, you think your place is bad, but believe me it's a palace. Sandra was telling me that they went to view a three-bedroom semi; it had tiny rooms, stank of damp and the décor was rank."

"That's horrible."

"Housing Benefit will pay most of the rent and Sandra's going to help out. You'll make £800 a month. You can pay for a room with that and have money over to cover the mortgage and live on, and Sandra's son and family get a home. Obviously they'll be responsible for bills and council tax. What do you think?" Charlotte finished triumphantly.

"Sounds great," Indigo felt a flutter of excitement within her. "I can't believe it. Everything's usually such hard work!"

"'What's for you, won't go against you', as my Granny used to say. He's a good lad, and he'll soon get another job anyway. I'll act as guarantor, so if they do prove unreliable you won't be in trouble."

"You are an angel!" 'Or, sent by the angels', Indigo thought.

The pieces of the puzzle that formed Indigo's life seemed finally to be fitting together. She was on the right path and focused, and things were beginning to happen for her. All she had to do now was sort herself out...

The evening stretched in front of her. She poured herself a glass of wine and sat on her rock seat looking out to sea. Her instinct was to get everything finalised as soon as possible. She texted Charlotte and told her that she was going to travel back the next day so that the young couple could come and see the house. If they liked it she would put some of the furniture into storage.

"Hey, you're still here." William jumped down onto the sand. "Wow, you're looking better. I was beginning to think that the pale, no make-up dishevelled look was your thing."

"Very funny."

"Boozing again I see," he checked his watch. "It's only just six o'clock. Do you have a drink problem?"

"It's only temporary... give me a bit of leeway."

"Hmm... heard that one before, but yeah, ok."

"You come to move me on?"

He smiled. His eyes were emerald in the sunlight.

"I should."

"One more day, officer, please? I can't move the van now anyway, I've been drinking."

"Aye. Disgusting!"

His radio crackled.

"Hang on..." He went back to the car. Returning, he handed her a piece of paper. "Just in case you do decide to invade Scotland, English. Here's a contact who may have a room to let. He's a decent old fella." He tilted his cap at her and left.

William's handwriting was neat and precise. Just like William. Indigo called the number on the piece of paper immediately, while she was still in a positive frame of mind. The gentleman's name was Wallace Cuthbert.

"PC MacLeod? Oh aye... He said about it did he? Yes, it's a good size room. £50 a week is the rent I want. That'd be ok would it?"

"Oh yes."

"I'll see you tomorrow at 9 a.m. then, Imogen."

"Indigo."

"What dear?"

"Yes, see you tomorrow." She smiled. He sounded old-school and pleasant.

Indigo wondered if William would return that evening or if she'd ever see him again. She mustn't think like that. That was her old self talking. No, this time in her life was about a fresh start that included healing, being on her own and discovering her spirituality. William was lovely, but probably married anyway. He was too gorgeous to be alone. Anyway, she was only interested in friendship. She couldn't cope with any demands on her emotions. She was too fragile.

At 8.55 the next morning, she arrived at Wallace Cuthbert's house. Turning through black wrought iron gates, the campervan trundled up a long leafy tunnel. Luscious trees lined the drive. Reaching a gravel area, Indigo saw a large Edwardian-style house with tall white windows. The lawns of the garden were immaculate. The black front door opened and out stepped a tall, distinguished, grey-haired man of about seventy.

Indigo walked up to him and shook his hand. His eyes were bright blue and full of life. His handshake was firm. He walked with the aid of a stick.

"Old war wound," he offered. "Shrapnel in my backside. Spent six months lying on my front."

Photographs of men in Navy uniforms lined the walls. Some sepia, others had been taken in the modern day.

"Falklands, not Second World War," he laughed. "I'm not that old."

The hallway boasted a chequered marble floor and winding staircase. Tasteful antique French furniture decorated the house.

"My wife had a liking for this type of furniture. Personally I prefer pure comfort. Your room is up the stairs, first door on your right. I can't make the stairs, so excuse my manners."

"No, that's fine. I'll just go and..." She pointed up the stairs.

"Yes, yes," he waved up the stairs. "Big kitchen downstairs. Modern. My son had it put in last year. My room's in the old lounge, easier that way. You may come and go as you please." He pointed to a large china teapot on the hallway table. "Rent goes in there every Friday, then we don't have the embarrassment of all that."

"Ok, great." Indigo started up the stairs.

The room was large and airy with French windows that opened out onto a balcony overlooking the sea. A dark oak four-poster bed dominated the room, dressed with clean white linen. The floors were bowed and creaked when she walked over to the large wardrobe that reminded her of something out of Narnia. Two doors led off from the bedroom. One opened to reveal a shiny new en-suite bathroom, the other to a dressing room. Indigo made her way downstairs.

"It's charming," she said. "I'd be delighted to take the room."

Wallace looked pleased and ushered her to the kitchen where a cup of tea was waiting.

"£50 for the room?" Indigo wanted to make sure.

"Is that too much?"

"No. Not at all. I didn't think it was enough actually."

"It's all I want for it," he said in a matter of fact way.

"I have to travel down to England today. But I will back up in a week. Is that ok? Do you want a deposit?"

"No, no. Just the first week's rent in the teapot on a Friday. If you rip me off I'll send PC MacLeod after you. His father served with me in the Navy." He chuckled at his joke and Indigo grinned.

"Thanks for the tea."

"You are most welcome." He handed her a key. "Pleasure to meet you, Imogen."

"Indigo."

The house was situated on the coastal road, just outside the main North Berwick town, near Tantallon Castle. Indigo turned left and joined the A1 to England. She had to deal with the past before she could head to the future. A task she was not looking forward to.

EIGHT
Initiation

By the time Indigo reached the M25 the old familiar blackness was beginning to churn in the pit of her belly. The sky was the colour of gunmetal grey. It matched her mood. Arriving in Canterbury an hour later she felt depressed and anxious, but her house looked back at her, friendly and full of happy memories of the children when they were growing up. The red, pink and cream roses that she had planted lined the garden fence. The long, dark green front lawn was overgrown and needed cutting. Historically, however, dark shadows lurked within her home for it had been a place of abuse for years at the hands of her ex-husband.

Unlocking the front door she picked up a few letters from the mat. Jeremy Clifford-Amos's handwriting was on one of the envelopes, large, blue and looping. She inhaled deeply. There was also a note from Mike. Their response to her actions could no longer be avoided. Mike's note read:

'Indigo, I thought I'd been burgled and nearly called the police. I still may have you arrested for vandalism. How dare you walk out on me like this! Where the hell are you? I was worried sick. Charlotte says you've gone away for a while and left your job. How irresponsible and selfish. What do you think you were doing and why? There's no excuse for your behaviour and you will pay. I want answers. Mike'

Indigo's legs gave way and she sank down to the floor, her heart beating rapidly. Mixed emotions of weariness, disappointment and regret rose within her. Tears of fear coursed down her cheeks. Mike had been so good for her in the beginning, boosting her confidence and making her feel sexy and alive, but she'd known subconsciously from the beginning that they were a mismatch and now this was the result of their failed friendship and all that had passed. It was painful and it hurt. Indigo cried for what could have been and for the finality of her relationship with him. For a moment she didn't think that she could bear it. She was a wretched creature, and worse, she had been a fool.

Under the circumstances, a confrontation would be horrendous. She was too fragile. Indigo hoped that she had got off lightly with an angry note. Screwing up the piece of paper, she chucked it across the kitchen. Dark demons were climbing her insides, sinking in their rancid talons. She bolted the doors. The curtains were already drawn.

Walking into the lounge she poured a large brandy from the crystal decanter on the dresser. Her nerves were shattered and she still had Clifford-Amos's letter to read. As if to deflect negative damage she texted Charlotte and told her that she had arrived back. Could the young couple come around tomorrow afternoon? Next she texted Rebecca and asked if she could have a session of Reiki the following day.

Clifford-Amos's letter was a rant, full of spelling mistakes. He was livid. She had cost him three quarters of a million pounds by not sending out the tender. He had no-one to run the office. Her resignation was illegal and a breach of contract. She was to call him immediately. Why had his emails been returned by the network with a 'no mailbox' notification? On and on it went. Indigo could imagine him standing there screaming at her with his bushy hair puffed out like candy floss and steam spouting from his ears. She ripped the letter into four pieces and threw it into the bin.

Her `phone bleeped twice. Charlotte and Rebecca had answered promptly. It was 'yes' to both of the texts and Charlotte warned her that she'd had a visit from Mike. The note must have been posted within the last few hours. She had an appointment for Reiki at 11 o'clock and the young couple would come round at 2 p.m. Pouring another brandy, Indigo emailed a storage company in the vicinity. Their rates were good and she'd heard that they were very efficient. Apparently they provided boxes and would collect the contents of the house.

Opening the windows at the back of the house, she wondered if it would be strange to live somewhere else. It had felt right in Scotland, but time would tell. The next few days would be difficult but then she'd be free. She had to focus on that. Images of the sea and her room at Wallace Cuthbert's came to mind. A warm glow temporarily eradicated murky fearfulness.

"The present is all there is," she said to herself. "Focus on that."

Draining her glass she told herself off for drinking so much. But as she'd said to William, it was just a temporary state. William seemed so far away. But she'd only seen him the day before. She wasn't sure which part of her life seemed unreal, her life in Kent or her time in Scotland. She decided that she was drunk. Throwing her clothes on the floor she crawled into bed, falling into a dreamless sleep.

Awaking at 8 o'clock with a raging thirst, she drank the pint of stale water by her bedside. Her stomach gurgled and popped with hunger and she realised that she had only eaten an egg mayonnaise roll the day before. The thought of food made her feel sick, but she managed a piece of toast and marmite and three cups of tea.

Entering the Canterbury Reiki Centre, Indigo could feel the warm positive energy soaking into her soul. Rebecca greeted her enthusiastically and they went straight to the treatment room where they sat in the seated area and talked for about half an hour.

"You're clearing all the negative aspects out of your life. Then you will be able to move on. All that you are going through is the universe showing you the way. You're on the right path. Often we have to lose a number of people along the way, people who suck our energy and are bad for us."

Indigo felt totally relaxed this time as she lay on the soft treatment table. Waves of heat and colour flowed through her, deep blue and purple, yellow, red and orange. She embraced the energy. Emerald hills, lochs and valleys and the image of someone came to her, but she could not see who it was, only feel the rich energy attached to them. Sitting up afterwards, she told Rebecca that it had been an uplifting but a less dramatic experience than before.

"Your energy is flowing better. Before, your chakras were all blocked."

"Do you have any space on the Reiki 1 training course this Friday? I know that it's a big thing on top of the move, but I think it might help."

Rebecca looked pleased.

"One space, yes. I think it will be good for you. I agree."

Indigo booked her place on the course. It was for one day from ten until four. Her plan was to travel back to Scotland on the Saturday. She was desperate to get everything finalised and move quickly before Mike turned up at her house, or Jeremy Clifford-Amos. It all seemed a massive rush, packing everything into a week. Some would consider her thoughtless or reckless, but Indigo knew that it had to happen at this pace and that she was a hundred per cent on the right path.

The young couple appeared at 2 p.m. He was tall and muscular with sandy short hair. She was small and blonde.

"Hi," said Indigo.

"Hi, I'm Tommy and this is Caitlin."

"Right, well come in and I'll show you round."

They had been looking for a house for months without luck and Tommy told her that the one place they'd found suitable, had refused them because he'd been made redundant. From their reaction it was apparent that they wanted to move in as soon as possible.

"We love it!" said Caitlin, her pretty face full of hope.

Shortly after they left, Charlotte `phoned her to confirm that Tommy and Caitlin definitely wanted to rent the house. Charlotte had experience of letting out houses to tenants and would sort out the legalities and other details. Indigo received a call from the storage company, and told them her requirements. They had a storage unit that was suitable, and to speed up the process she drove to the depot to collect seventy cardboard boxes. There was a lot to do. The removal men were coming to put her belongings into storage on Saturday morning.

By Thursday, Tommy and Caitlin had signed the tenancy agreement, and Charlotte was officially acting as their guarantor. Indigo spent the week packing. All the belongings she wanted to take with her were loaded into the campervan.

On Friday morning she arrived back at the Reiki Centre. Despite spending the week immersed in positive activities she felt uncertain and nervous about completing the Reiki 1 course. The week had been an anxious one. She'd been terrified that Mike would appear on her doorstep. She knew him well, and was unnerved by the fact that he hadn't. It made her wonder what he was plotting. Furthermore, Jeremy Clifford-Amos's letter had upset her immensely and she was fearful of his possible actions against her.

Entering Reception she felt relieved and grounded. Her panic subsided; anxiety dispersed. Suddenly everything made sense once more. The murmur of voices came from upstairs and this time instead of venturing through the mysterious door she headed up the stairs into a large, airy and light studio with gleaming wooden floorboards. Large windows lined the walls and a table was set up containing coffee, tea and snacks. Chairs had been placed in a circle. A Reiki treatment table lay over to the far left. There were three other women in the room as well as Rebecca.

"This is Alice, Mary and Elizabeth. This is Indigo," said Rebecca.

"Hi." Indigo smiled.

They sat down and Rebecca handed out some course booklets. The first exercise was to get into pairs and talk about the spiritual aspect of their lives and why they wanted to do the course. Afterwards they would give a summary to the group of what their partner had divulged. Indigo paired up with Alice.

"Right... who goes first?" said Alice.

"You can. If that's ok."

"Yes, ok. Right, well, I'm Alice and I work in a school with children with special needs. My husband's just retired and is at home all the time, and my life is tiring and I need something for myself. I've always been interested in spiritual healing, the supernatural, that kind of thing. A friend of mine recommended the Reiki Centre to me. That's about it."

"Have you had Reiki before?" asked Indigo.

"Yes, I have. It was wonderful. It made me feel more focused, aware and more energetic. How about you?"

"A couple of times, yes. Do you find it different with your husband at home?"

"Yes, I mean I work quite a lot of the day, but he's demanding and still expects me to do everything for him. The kids at the school are lovely, but it's not an easy job. I just feel like I have spent years giving and I want something different for the rest of my life. What about you? Have you had any spiritual experiences?"

"I'm not sure, kind of. I've always been interested in some other power. When I was a child I would lay on my back on the grass and spend hours looking up at the stars and the universe trying to work out what life and the world was all about. My main thing was to try to work out infinity, what was outside of the outside of the outside. It used to drive me mad, and make me feel insignificant. I realise now that I should have realised I had a big part to play in it all, but I was too young and didn't know anything. I just had feelings, sensations, intuitions - and vivid dreams. The problem is, I still feel insignificant a lot of the time, despite being an adult now."

"Yes, I know that feeling well." Alice leant forward and patted Indigo's hand. "Is that what brought you here, the desire for answers?"

"Not really, although I guess it was a factor. I'm not sure. I've had a bit of a rough time lately with ex-partners and work and I saw an advertisement for Reiki and thought that it would be good for me. I was having problems coping with the negative people in my life – I guess my life needed some healing. I was brought up as a Christian and I do believe in spiritual healing. But I'm not keen on anything to do with the supernatural or things like that. It's not my thing. Find all that a bit scary."

After the introductory exercise they learnt a little about the origins of Reiki, the founder Mikao Usui and other teachers of various traditions. At coffee break Indigo chatted to the other women and flicked through the self-help and Reiki books laid out on the table. She had read a couple of them.

Rebecca gave a brief talk about what to expect at the attunement ceremony then the class ventured individually downstairs to the Reiki treatment room for the attunement. Indigo went first. She sat down in a chair and pressed her palms together. Rebecca moved her hands over her and called Reiki to Indigo. She felt a powerful energy surging throughout her being and the swirling of colours. It was a similar sensation to her first Reiki session but stronger. She cupped her hands as instructed and Rebecca placed within her palms a rose quartz crystal, and soon the ceremony finished. Indigo returned upstairs and wrote some notes on her pad, about how she'd experienced a positive forceful energy, and that she felt quite spaced-out but buzzing with energy. Then she slouched down in her seat. Closing her eyes she absorbed the Reiki while waiting for the rest of the group.

After the last member of the group had returned, Rebecca came in smiling. She wanted them to practise Reiki as a group, and tell her what they were experiencing. Alice, seated on Indigo's right, shut her eyes and meditated for a moment before calling Reiki to her. She sat in silence for about five minutes and then with excitement told the group how she'd seen an angel. It was a very special spiritual experience for her, quite beautiful. But it frightened Indigo. Spirituality was not yet a part of her everyday life, and she was in a delicate personal place. An intense, overwhelming heat was building within her. Indigo was terrified of the gift of Reiki that she'd received. Not ungrateful, but fearful. She looked at Rebecca and left the room, muttering that she felt a bit unwell.

Reaching the cool sanctuary of Reception, she put her head in her hands and cried. The atmosphere upstairs was extreme with multiple energies, it had overwhelmed her. She was sure that she was picking up on the emotional states of the others. It was too much for her. Chastising herself for being over-emotional, she fanned herself with one of the magazines on the coffee table, trying to cool down. After ten minutes Rebecca came down to see if she was ok.

"Indigo, you are vibrating on a higher level than most and this is why you feel things so intensely. Reiki is good. It comes from love and therefore can do you no harm. When I call it, it comes from a higher source. From the angels."

Indigo went to the bathroom and then back upstairs. The other women just smiled, as if simply accepting that everyone is affected differently by life's experiences. How she wished she could be like them.

After a lunch of rocket, tomatoes with French dressing, small vegetarian pasties, and green tea with pomegranate, they got ready for the practical aspect of the course. They would each lie on the treatment table and give Reiki to one another. After her earlier emotional departure, Indigo volunteered her services first. She cleared her mind and called Reiki, holding her hands over Elizabeth in the correct hand positions. She made an effort to concentrate, in order to clear any blockages and to remember the location of the chakras.

Doubt filled her as she wondered if anything was actually happening. Her mind kept drifting off to everyday matters, like should she take any shopping with her the next day, and then back to the healing power. In her present psychological state, concentration was not her forte. Elizabeth mentioned that she could feel a strong heat radiating from Indigo's hands especially onto her face and that reassured her.

Rebecca commented that even if the practitioner or client doesn't feel an overwhelming sensation, Reiki is still working and effective. Next, Mary practised on Indigo, and she felt the heat of Reiki and it felt good, although it wasn't as strong as what she received from Rebecca. Afterwards, they removed their shoes and sat in a circle with their eyes shut. The course was to be brought to a close with creative visualisation.

♦ ♦ ♦

They were taken down some stairs, through a door that led to a beautiful beach where the sand was white. The sea glittering emerald and the sky was a dark blue. There were green palm trees swaying in a cool breeze. A tall, white, frothing waterfall poured churning fresh water into a leafy crystal lagoon below. Here they could be themselves and let go of any inhibitions that possessed them. Here they could be free. It was an inner sanctuary. Indigo found herself dancing along the beach like a child, full of life with a sense of ultimate freedom. The place was pure, and free from the stresses of life.

Later, when they were ready to go, they journeyed back through the door and up the stairs to a golden chamber. They sat on Persian rugs laden with soft cushions and let a brilliant gold and glittering healing light flow from the heavens through their crown chakras filling their entire body, soaking into every part of them. Indigo could see the golden light filling her.

She could see an eye, and wondered whether it was her own third eye or the opening of the crown chakra, as it seemed to alternate between both. One moment she saw a vivid eye, the next an opening like body tissue, eye-shaped, similar to the vagina. Strong golden energy pulsed through her until she felt weightless and powerful. Slowly Rebecca brought them back to consciousness. They came out of the chamber and moved slowly back up the stairs.

◆ ◆ ◆

The group sat in silence for a few moments and then gradually came to. Sitting chatting, they drank glasses of water, each treasuring their own personal experience. Four o'clock came and it was time to go home.

"This has been a really nice group. Congratulations to you all. You may now practise self-healing, also on family or friends. It is after Reiki level two that you can begin to give healing to others." She smiled at Alice. "Have I answered your questions, Alice?"

"Yes. I've really enjoyed today."

The others in the group muttered the same.

"I'm delighted. Well, blessings to you all and I hope to see you back here for Reiki level two."

It had been a very different experience for Indigo but it was one that she would cherish for her entire life. She was proud of the gift that had been given to her and eternally grateful.

Indigo checked around the house on the Friday evening to ensure that everything was in order for the removal company. All the items to be put into storage were clearly labelled. There was just one last box full of shoes and boots to go into the camper-van. She went out to put them in, and locked the van. Suddenly, her stomach began to churn and a feeling of bleakness came over her. Turning she saw Mike standing on the pavement glaring at her. Her first instinct was to bolt back to the house, but he blocked her way.

"Get in the house, and go quietly," he snarled under his breath. Dressed in a dark grey shirt with jeans, his blue eyes were cold and held no emotion.

Indigo's legs began to shake as she turned back to the house. Closing the door behind them, Mike ran his fingers through his hair and stood with his hands on his hips. For a moment he just stared at her saying nothing. Then, he took a folded piece of paper out of his back pocket.

"I've made a list of how much you cost me. First there's the housekeeping – none was bought. Ruined food, heating bill, toilet paper," he brandished the paper, "inconvenience and mess," he roared, taking a menacing step towards her. "And you think that you've left me! A stupid, insignificant, middle-aged tart! How dare you?"

He grabbed hold of her hair and bent her head back.

"I'll pay you back, Mike," she whispered.

"Yes, you will," he said, his face pressed up close to hers.

Indigo felt the full extent of his wrath as his fists punished her. She remembered the dream where she'd had the out of body experience and again hoped that it was not her time to die as she was just beginning to enjoy living once more. She prayed to the angels for divine intervention. It may have been a coincidence but just then a loud bleeping sounded from outside. His car alarm had gone off. Mike had been in the process of undoing his jeans, he swore with rage. Looking down at Indigo's crumpled crying form lying on the stairs he glanced out of the window at his car. A ginger cat was running from the scene with its tail down and ears back.

"Bloody cats have set the damn alarm off," he spat. "I'll give you a few days to think how you're going to pay me back. I'm not sure if I'll take you back after this." He left, slamming the door behind him.

Indigo staggered stiffly to her feet. She went to the bathroom and ran a bath. Her body was covered in bruises and by tomorrow she would look as if she'd been in a boxing match. Half of her face was swollen, red and stinging. Fortunately, the confrontation had taken place in the hallway. The lounge door had been closed and Mike hadn't seen the packed cardboard boxes. She hoped that he was ignorant of her plans to move. This wasn't the first time that she'd suffered physical abuse. Her ex-husband had done the same. What was it about her? She winced as she lowered herself into the soothing, cleansing hot water. It was her old self that attracted negative suckers who drained the energy of others. The Indigo of today would recognise these people in time and they wouldn't be allowed near her. Silently, she thanked the higher powers for saving her at a crucial moment.

NINE

The Healing Begins

Indigo arrived back in Scotland late the next evening. Feeling battered and worn she glanced at her watch. It was ten o'clock. During the past week, she'd utilised every waking minute and now after a nine-hour drive from Canterbury to North Berwick she felt completely exhausted. Wallace Cuthbert came out to greet her. Indigo took one look at his friendly welcoming face and felt like bursting into tears. He noticed her bruised face but said nothing. She decided to unpack the campervan the following day, and after a brief cup of tea headed upstairs to her room. Climbing into the clean crisp bed sheets, she pulled up the duvet, and closed her eyes.

"Let the healing begin," she muttered. She felt safe.

The bed was extremely soft and comfortable and Indigo slept deeply throughout the night. She awoke early, about eight a.m., with the sun streaming in through a crack in the red curtains. Padding across the thick cream carpet, she opened the French windows. A blast of sea air entered the room. The silence of the house was filled with the sound of seagulls squawking shrilly overhead and the waves battering against the cliffs in the distance. The view of the bay was perfect, like a seascape. The deep blue North Sea stretched out endlessly touching the horizon, volcanic islands adding mystery to the scene. Fields filled with wild flowers of orange, blue and purple lay to her right. North Berwick, and the far away hills of Fife across the water, were to her left. The sky was a light blue with a smattering of clouds.

Throwing on her white dressing gown, Indigo tiptoed down the marble stairs feeling the cold stone under her bare feet. There was no-one about and Wallace's car was absent from the gravel parking area outside. He'd mentioned to her that he was hardly ever at home as he was an active member of the local bowling club and sat on various committees. Filling her flask with tea, she returned to her room. There was a soft wooden garden bench out on the balcony and she sat out there. It was a cool morning and she wrapped herself in a blanket. Sipping her tea, she reflected on what she had achieved in just a week. It was amazing what could be done when the focus was there. It had helped that the angels seemed to have ensured that her transition from her old life in England to her new one in Scotland went smoothly. She couldn't have done any of it without Charlotte. She must remember to send her some flowers. She refused to think about the altercation with Mike the previous day. He would not be allowed to pollute her present.

Firing up her laptop, she clicked onto the Internet. Thankfully, Wallace's son seemed to be up to date with everything from shiny new bathrooms and modern kitchens to wireless broadband. He'd made sure that his father had everything he needed, whether he wanted it or not. She wondered idly whether Wallace's wife had died. He'd mentioned her a couple of times, but he hadn't looked sad or hinted that she had.

There was an email from the Reiki Centre, a mailshot listing holistic therapies and spiritual events from psychic readings and aura recognition to a list of spiritual retreats. Scrolling down the list, she mused that the warm embrace of the Centre would be missed; but she planned to complete her Reiki 2 at some point in the future and would keep in contact with Rebecca.

'Discover your spirituality on a Spiritual Healing Retreat...' Clicking onto the link she saw that these were being held in a variety of locations from Worcester in England to the Isle of Mull in Scotland and Santa Fe in the USA. Immediately she moved the mouse to Isle of Mull and the page opened.

The Isle of Mull Healing Centre was advertising a spiritual healing weekend retreat, to be held in just a couple of weeks. The centre offered en-suite rooms within a vast Georgian mansion situated in the beautiful grounds of a Scottish estate. The website photographs showed rooms sparsely furnished with a bed, wardrobe and dressing-table, but the furniture was solid oak. A flat screen TV with a built-in DVD player hung from the wall. The floors were red flagstone covered with rustic rugs. White linen curtains framed the tall windows and the general impression was one of quality. There was a heated indoor pool, Jacuzzi, sauna and treatment rooms for massage and other holistic therapies with a wealth of thick fluffy cream towels and leafy dark green plants. It all looked luxurious.

There were walled peace gardens, outdoor hot tubs, lakes dotted with lily pads, waterfalls, fountains and statues. An abundance of colourful flowers filled the grounds. The walled areas led to green leafy glades, dark enchanted woods and vast yellow meadows full of long grasses, wild flowers, bees and butterflies.

Glancing at the price list Indigo saw that the prices for the three-day retreat were quite reasonable; then she realised that she hadn't read the details properly. Going back to the booking form, she saw that people attending the retreat would be camping in the grounds. 'Mother Earth would assist them in their quest to discover their spirituality and tune in to their higher selves'. They would be responsible for putting up their own tents, building a fire, cooking food and they would need to use the small loch for washing themselves and their dishes. There would be group meditation and exercise, counselling and discussion. There would also be a camp fire in the evenings with music. Indigo smiled. A reckless feeling came over her and she filled out the booking form, paying the deposit with her credit card. There was a small one-man tent in the campervan. It would be fun and relaxing and she might meet some new people. The day had started off well.

"All I have is this moment and all is well, so that's good," she said, wincing as she shifted position. Her body was sore.

A white van trundled up the drive, crunching onto the gravelled area as it came to a halt. Indigo's room was to the side of the house overlooking the sea but she still had a view of the grounds at the front. A man of about five foot ten stepped out of the vehicle. He was muscular with short dark hair, dressed in old jeans, builder's boots and a black heavy metal t-shirt. Opening the back of the van he rummaged inside before pulling out a lawn mower, strimmer and spade. Turning, he pulled the wire out from the mower and plugged it into the outside electrical socket. Indigo gasped. There was no mistaking those looks. It was William.

Instinctively, she sat back and checked if he could see her from where he was. Then it occurred to her that he was a policeman, observant and aware. He would have already noted a figure sitting on the balcony as he drove up the drive. Plus he had recommended Wallace Cuthbert to her and therefore would know that she had moved in. Naturally, Indigo should go downstairs and say hello, but she felt flustered by his arrival. She liked him and wanted to see him, but at the same time he disturbed her. If she ignored him she would appear odd or rude. Even though her energy was low, she still should make the effort to be friendly. After all, if he hadn't made the effort to give her Wallace's details she would not be sitting here today.

A confirmation email arrived from Isle of Mull Healing Centre. They thanked her for the online booking and were looking forward to seeing her. Indigo logged onto the national florist site that she used and sent Charlotte two dozen carnations of cream, pink and red as they were her favourite flowers. The note was to say simply: 'Thank you. Love, Indigo x.'

The sound of the lawn mower starting up shattered the tranquillity. Indigo moved from the balcony to the bathroom where she took a power shower. Dressing in jeans and a long-sleeved white t-shirt, she applied make-up. The long sleep had done her good. She took her dirty flask down to the kitchen to wash up and make some coffee, muttering to herself 'be normal'. When she opened the front door, William cut the power and turned around smiling. She had been correct in her assumption. He had been aware of her and knew that she'd moved in.

"Did I wake you?" he asked. The next minute his face darkened. "What's happened to you?"

"Nothing to worry about," she smiled nervously. "Slipped carrying a box downstairs. You think I look bad, the contents of the box were smashed to bits."

"Aye." William sounded unconvinced and his eyes flashed. "You're ok now?"

She'd forgotten how attractive he was. It was strange. She felt really comfortable with him as though she could tell him anything but at the same time his presence made her feel a little awkward and shy. She nodded.

THE HEALING BEGINS

"Yes, bit bruised but fine. No, you didn't wake me. I was dealing with some emails."

"You arrived back yesterday?"

She nodded.

"Would you like some coffee, William?"

"Aye, white, one sugar."

He started up the mower without a word of explanation as to why a full-time policeman should be working as a gardener for Wallace Cuthbert. Returning to the kitchen she made some instant Brazilian coffee and took two cups outside. There were old stone steps leading down to the front lawn and they sat there.

"Well, here you are," he said, taking a gulp of his coffee.

"Aye," said Indigo, "here I am."

"That's a dreadful attempt at a Scottish accent, English." He turned and looked at her.

"Let's hear you do an English one then?"

"Aff a pand of apples an pears," he said in a cockney accent, and then changed to upper class English. "It's frightfully good to meet you again, Ms Summers, jolly pleased."

Indigo laughed. The accent completely changed his character.

"You should be on the stage."

"Not me. Too shy." He gave her a wicked grin.

"Have you ever been to England?"

"Twice to London. It's nice, but Scotland's my home despite the rain."

"Did you go there for a holiday?"

"No. A woman, an English girl. It was my turn to visit her, that was all."

"Did you marry her?"

"No. It wasn't serious. Just sex really."

Indigo didn't know what to say.

"He's ok, the old man." William inclined his head towards the house.

"Yes, really nice. Did his wife die?"

William raised his eyebrows.

"It's no secret. She had, has, a liking for men, lots of men. There is no man on earth who could satisfy her."

"Blimey."

"Aye. After numerous lovers, she took him for half of everything and did one with a toy boy, twenty years younger. She got bored of him too after a year. Last thing Wallace heard she was living in France with a Count."

"Dracula?"

"About the same age, but your geography is out. He was from Transylvania."

"Are you surprised I moved up?"

William looked out to sea. His vivid green eyes were lively but guarded. He was silent for so long that Indigo thought that he was ignoring her.

"No. I'm not," he said finally. "When I first met you I thought you were a crackhead or something, then I realised quickly that you were simply exhausted by your life in England." He drained his mug. "I'm not surprised that you dug deep and found the strength to change your life. I would have been more surprised if you hadn't."

He handed her the empty cup that was still hot from the drink.

"Thanks. What now, Indigo?"

"I've booked a spiritual retreat on the Isle of Mull in a few weeks. Until then I guess I'll just try to recover from everything. Get myself fit."

William grinned.

"Spiritual retreat?"

"It's a healing retreat."

"Of course. You look like you could do with it." He trailed his finger lightly along the angry purple marks on her wrist. "I run most days, along the coastal paths. I'm plugged into my iPod, but you can come if you want."

"Ok. I'm not that fit though."

"You can follow me, then. I'll call for you at five-thirty."

"Ok," she nodded.

"In the morning."

Starting up the mower, he turned his back on her. Indigo sat for a while watching his muscles ripple beneath his clothes as he moved the mower across the grass. She still knew nothing about his history apart from the fact that he worked for East Lothian police, had slept with a girl from London, cut Wallace's grass, ran and took coffee white with one sugar.

TEN

Running On

Indigo set her alarm for 5 a.m. Crawling out of bed, she glanced at her naked reflection in the long mirror. She had a good figure, slim with a fair size bust. Her fitness levels were reasonable but needed improvement. Her body was a mess of black, red and purple bruising around her arms, ribs and collarbone. It was ridiculous that Mike had beaten her, thought nothing of it and walked away. If a stranger had inflicted these injuries they would have been arrested for assault. What was worse was the fact that it hadn't even occurred to her to call the police and have him arrested. Deep down, she must have thought that she deserved it. William would not be impressed if he saw the state of her. He hadn't believed the story about her falling down the stairs. He'd probably heard that particular lame excuse numerous times before from an array of poor battered woman and maybe even men.

She applied some light make-up, and tied her long dark hair back into a pony tail, releasing some tendrils on one side to help cover the sore side of her face. Foundation covered it a little but the bruise had spread and had changed from red to purple. Dressing in pink jogging bottoms, t-shirt and tracksuit top she put her iPod in her zipped-up pocket and ran down the stairs to make a coffee.

They walked to the end of the rose garden, through a gate and down a stony track framed by long wet wild grasses. The track met up with the coastal path that wound for miles around East Lothian. William was wearing a tracksuit and trainers with a small sports backpack. After stretching their arm and leg muscles they began jogging slowly along the path. Indigo trotted after him managing to keep up well until she realised that this was just his warm-up. As his speed increased she fell back, she was already out of breath. As he sped around a corner, she stopped, gasping for air. She could see him at the bottom of the track looking to see where she'd got to. She waved him on. He began running across the sand. She recognised his athletic gait. He was the runner she'd seen on the beach during her first night in North Berwick with the campervan, she was sure of it. Taking a long drink of water, she ran down the track onto the sand, moving to the hard compact area that had been left behind by the deserting tide.

William was incredibly fit. Indigo wasn't. After a slow run along half of the length of the beach, her legs began to resemble leaden jelly and she managed a mild jog. By the time she reached the Seabird Centre at the end of the first beach, her jog had become a fast stroll. It was all she could manage. William had already run past the Centre along to the end of the other beach and was on his way back. He was perspiring as he ran up to her.

He took a large bottle of water from his rucksack and drained half of it.

"First effort English, don't be too bothered about being thrashed by a superior Scotsman!" He laughed, wiping his face with a hand towel, and she realised that she'd never heard him laugh before. It was a deep throaty sound. "I suppose you're wiped out... or are you?"

"I'm ok," Indigo smiled. "Just pacing myself."

"Aye. You won't be up for training tomorrow then?"

"I will."

"Swimming tomorrow in an icy loch." He put his towel and water bottle back in his backpack. "You can swim?"

Indigo was a strong swimmer.

"Yes, I'll thrash you!" Suddenly she remembered the bruises. She would wear a t-shirt over her swimsuit. That would cover most of them.

"What's the matter?"

"Nothing."

His eyes searched hers.

"Come on, English. Race you back!"

She ran after him. Returning to Wallace Cuthburt's he said goodbye and went off to work. Indigo felt exhausted. She took a shower and went back to bed.

The following morning dawned. Opening the curtains at 5 a.m. she was greeted by white mist and torrential rain. Their swim would be cancelled. Returning to bed she fell asleep. Moments later there was a knocking on her bedroom door. She awoke with a jump.

"English?" William's voice came from outside the door.

Groggily she sat up in bed. Her bedroom door opened. William stood there in his tracksuit.

"Are you ill?"

"It was raining!"

He smiled incredulously at her.

"You're in Scotland, English. What do you think we're made of up here? Up you get! I'll turn my back."

He turned around theatrically.

"Swimsuit, towel, hairbrush and tracksuit. Add a warm jumper. I've got a large flask of hot chocolate."

Indigo climbed out of bed and disappeared into the dressing room. Leaving the door open she undressed and put on her swimsuit and other clothing.

"Do I get a coffee?"

"No time. You should've got up as arranged."

"It was raining. It is raining!"

"If I was gonna cancel, I'd have told you."

"You should've been a sergeant major in the army," she grumbled, following him outside. He gestured to his white van and she got in.

"Who says I wasn't?" he retorted.

Indigo looked at his side profile. She wasn't sure yet when he was joking. He started the ignition and handed her a flask.

"Have a drink."

They drove for about ten minutes. Indigo sipped the hot chocolate trying not to throw the hot liquid down the neck of her t-shirt. Each time she went to take a sip the van seemed to bounce over a bump in the road. Eventually, they drove up to a set of white gates. William punched in a set of numbers and the gates opened automatically. Woodland lay on either side of the drive. A large house similar to Cuthbert Wallace's loomed in the distance. William continued past the house until they reached a large loch that stretched for about half a mile.

"What is this place William?"

"This is where I grew up," said William. "It's my parents' house. Now, we're five minutes behind, so quick."

Indigo gazed at the loch with apprehension. It was surrounded by dark green forest and was both intimidating and primitive. Frosty rain punctured the smooth surface with a million tiny pin pricks. The water was black. God only knew what was lurching in the freezing depths. William had already left the van and stripped off down to his swimming shorts. He had the physique of a gymnast. Strong shoulders, developed biceps, a six-pack and tapered waist. His legs were muscular and strong. Flexing his muscles, he banged on her window.

"Out."

Hesitantly, she opened the door.

"I'll undress in here so that my dry clothes don't get wet."

Indigo stripped down to her swimsuit but left her t-shirt on. She stepped out of the van.

"That'll weigh you down, English. Get it off." William tugged at her t-shirt jokingly. Indigo looked at him defensively. The atmosphere changed and he stepped back. "Seriously, it will. I'm sorry, I wasn't being smutty." He looked down for a moment, embarrassed.

Indigo didn't know what to do. If she took the t-shirt off, then he would know that the bruises hadn't been caused by an accident. But he knew that anyway. She felt mortified. She felt like going off in a mood to avoid the situation, but William would be upset and their friendship would be tainted.

She took the t-shirt off and heard his intake of breath. It was a pity that it wasn't because he'd seen her magnificent body for the first time. Instead, it was a reaction to the tale of Mike's wrath that coloured her body like an obscene oil painting. Indigo didn't know how to deal with his eyes taking in the hurt inflicted by the past. For a moment his eyes left her body and met hers. His were full of questions and anger. Hers held the need for avoidance.

"Come on, you great stuffed haggis," she called.

Indigo, filled with nervous adrenalin, chucked her clothes into the car and ran to the edge of the loch. Plunging into the cold, she gasped. Laughing, she struck out and began to swim strongly. The loch was about a half a mile in width and length. William followed her trying to catch her up. Reaching the middle of the loch, she turned onto her back. William passed her and motored to the far side. Rolling onto her front, she swam to where he was.

"Race you," she challenged and set off before he could answer.

He passed her just half-way, and to add insult greeted her with a towel as she reached the other side. Indigo emerged from the freezing water shaking with cold. He placed the towel with exaggerated gentleness around her shoulders. She didn't want to tell him about the past. It was important that he knew her for who she was as a person, not by what had happened to her. Maybe one day, but not now.

William had already put the heater on in the van. Closing the doors they sat in the warmth drinking steaming hot chocolate listening to the rain pelting on the roof. Huge droplets streamed down the glass. The windscreen began to steam up. William flicked the windscreen heater and wipers on.

"Lovely summer we're having. You're a good swimmer."

"Thanks," Indigo grinned.

"I actually had to exert myself to catch you up!"

"Oh did you!"

"Seriously, I was impressed by your swimming." His eyes twinkled.

"Good job or I might have drowned out there."

He smiled.

"I doubt you'd have drowned. If you'd got into difficulty you could have stood on the slimy bottom. The loch's shallow. The water'll come up to your chin!"

"Oh, you kept that quiet. I'm a bit out of condition at the moment, but I've always swum so it won't take long. I'll soon be out-pacing you."

William chuckled.

"Deluded English..." He dried his hair with a white towel. Glancing at his watch, he sighed. "Time to go... as always!"

Indigo glanced at him. His dark hair was swept back, and his long eyelashes were still wet and stuck together. The swim had been exhilarating and his green eyes shone.

"Shall I drop you off like that or do you want to get changed?"

"No, I'll be straight in the shower." She stuffed her tracksuit into the small rucksack.

"I'm on early shift tomorrow and for the next week... covering for a mate. So I won't be able to continue with this for now... maybe cycling one evening?"

"Yeah, ok. I'll see if I can get hold of a bike."

William gave her his police business card with his mobile number on it.

"Text me if you get one."

Wallace greeted her in the hallway. As an ex-navy man, he seemed to think that swimming in a loch early in the morning was normal behaviour. Lying in bed until mid-day for him would be odd.

"We thought we might go cycling," said Indigo standing on the marble floor wrapped in a towel. "But I don't have a bike."

"The wife left hers. Only used it twice. Might be a bit old-fashioned with three gears..."

"You'd be happy for me to use it?"

"Of course. It's in the out-building. The one at the end. Help yourself. Got to dash," he checked his watch, "breakfast meeting. On the agenda, should a crazy golf course be put next to the putting green – crucial stuff!"

Indigo grinned. Wallace loved being busy. After her shower she wolfed down bacon and eggs followed by two cups of hot coffee. The bike was, as Wallace said, virtually brand new. Indigo wiped off the dust and decided to take it for a spin. The rain had stopped although the day was grey. She rode down the long drive crossing the main road. Turning down a sleepy country lane with overgrown hedgerows, she gradually became used to the move-ment of the bicycle and started to enjoy the ride. The hills loomed in the distance, dark and mysterious like rustic patch-work. One to the forefront was illuminated gold by the sun peeping through a tiny gap in the thick cloud. Standing alone it glowed in contrast to the others. Stopping for a drink of water, she texted William. He'd be pleased that she managed to find a bike so soon.

Returning home, she picked up her forwarded mail from the Post Office redirection service. There was a letter from Mike. She recognised his handwriting and her stomach plummeted with fright. Then her mobile `phone bleeped. It was William.

'Hi. Sorry but really busy at work, two off sick. Good that you've got a bike. Talk soon. W.'

Indigo looked from the letter to the `phone and back again. Happiness fell away from her, leaving the familiar sensation of loneliness and fear. Then she felt annoyed with herself. This was a fresh start and yet her moods were still being affected by outside forces and people. She needed to think. Grabbing a bottle of red wine, she took a plastic picnic wine glass and pulled on her wellies, thick padded coat and hat. Striding past the yellow, pink and white roses nodding in the breeze she opened the gate and headed for the coastal path. The cliffs graduated down to the light grey sea and sandy cove below. Leaving the track she clambered down the black slate.

Hidden from view by the cliff tops, she found a seat in the rock and poured herself a glass of wine. She was trying so hard to stay positive and focused, administering the self-healing Reiki daily and making sure that she kept herself grounded and protected. So why did it feel as though everything was falling apart?

The letter throbbed with bad vibrations within her pocket. She should burn it without reading it. But, taking a deep breath, she tore it open.

'Indigo, I hear from Charlotte that you've moved away...' Indigo drained the wine glass as she read the list of expletives relating to her. 'My last punishment was nothing to what will happen to you if I ever lay eyes on you again. You better not set foot in Canterbury again.'

The threats and character assassination continued, and Indigo scanned the letter before refolding it. Should she keep it or burn it? If she destroyed it and something happened to her there would be no evidence to tie him to the crime. He obviously had no idea where she had gone or he would have made some scathing reference. How she hated him. Blackness churned within her and she drained her second glass of wine. Negative thoughts spread as they sped to a ripe environment for rapid breeding. Mike's face loomed up in her mind. Bad temper consumed her and after the third glass of wine she snapped.

"I hate you,' she screamed at the letter. "You've ruined everything, again. You've polluted me. Ruined my life, my Reiki experience, my positive energy. You pathetic sadistic monster! I loathe and detest you! I curse you to hell and hope that pain is inflicted upon you. That you suffer!"

The letter had pushed Indigo into a flat spin. As she began to cry, tears dropped onto her bruised wrists, another reminder of his cruelty. She had lost her grounding. The sky had darkened to gunmetal grey. The sea reflected the mood. She didn't want to return home, her restless mood required fresh air and nature. However, the weather dictated otherwise. Turning, she stood up, above her head over to the left was a small indent in the cliff face. She had time to investigate before the rain came. Scrambling up the slate she saw that it was a small cave. It offered shelter as it was deep and positioned practically at the top of the cliff. Flicking on her lighter, she saw that there was quite a bit of room in there and no apparent wild creatures. She'd brought the lighter and a candle to burn Mike's letter.

Indigo marvelled at how quickly the weather had changed. The whole world seemed shrouded in blackness and sea mist. She'd been so engrossed in her thoughts that she hadn't noticed. A bang of thunder like cannon fire sounded overhead, shaking the cliffs. Flashes of brilliant white light and zigzags of silver forked lightning danced across the rolling ocean towards her.

"Shit!"

Indigo scrambled into the cave and sat near the back. She'd have to wait until the storm passed. Large droplets of rain splashed onto the rocks. The waves heaved uncontrollably, casting eight-foot walls of spray up against the slate walls that jutted out seaward. The rain was torrential, bouncing off the black shiny surface. A crack of thunder sounded again. Fork lightning struck the sandy cove below like an angry snake striking at its prey. Indigo gazed at the sheer force of nature with a mixture of wonder and horror. Her mobile `phone rang. Indigo looked at it dumbly. It didn't fit into the scene unfolding in front of her eyes.

She was tempted to ignore it, but it might be important. It was eight o'clock; where had the time gone? Her brain was fuddled by stress, wine and negativity.

"Hi, Charlotte."

"Hi," Charlotte's tone sounded serious. "Indigo, got some bad news."

"What?" Dread filled her.

"Thomas has called me from work. Mike's been in a traffic accident."

74

Pure ice seeped into every cell in her body from her crown to the tip of her toes.

"Is he dead?" Indigo's earlier curse hovered like a bubble in her mind.

"No, unconscious. He's broken his hand and leg. Bit of a painful break. There's a head wound, too. Thomas said the next hour is crucial, if he survives that then he'll make it."

"Thanks for letting me know."

"Hope you're ok, Indigo?"

"Yeah, thanks. Let me know."

Indigo was numb with shock. Had she caused the accident? Pouring a fourth glass of wine she called Rebecca. The rain increased in volume but she was dry and safe within her cave. In a gush she told her what had happened.

"Did I cause it?" Indigo demanded.

"Reiki comes from a place of love. It doesn't operate like that, Indigo. You're talking about dark witchcraft. Reiki is a healing power only."

"What if it's triggered some kind of psychic ability?"

"That's not possible. Indigo, it's just a coincidence, that's all. You told me once when we were talking that Mike often drives at a frightening speed."

"But he broke his hand," insisted Indigo.

"Did he kick you the other night?"

"No."

"But he also broke his leg in a couple of places," Rebecca reasoned. "You're distraught. You've been through a horrendous ordeal and you have mixed feelings. This is not your responsibility. This is not your journey. It's his. Distance yourself. His accident has everything to do with his life and energy and nothing to do with yours."

"Ok." Relief flooded Indigo. Her conscience was clear.

"You need to ground and protect yourself, do some Reiki self-healing. Keep positive. You've gone into a negative spin. This is normal. You're still in transition."

"Thanks, Rebecca."

Indigo sat looking out at the storm. The power was decreasing and the thunder and lightning travelled to other lands. She felt a little drunk. Her padded jacket was thermal and the temperature wasn't low and so she felt comfortable. How would she feel if he died? Sad for him, she supposed. If he survived she hoped that he would learn from the accident and reflect upon the way he conducted himself.

She thought about the dreams that had visited her over the past couple of months. The out of body experience and the barren wasteland dream depicted her past life and informed her of the need for change. The spiritual healer dream was to guide her away from her stale existence and show her a new way to live; and the basement dream told her that she was a worthwhile person with a beautiful soul. She consisted of different dimensions. She must have faith and move forward.

Her `phone woke her later with the bleep of a text message. It was Charlotte.

'Out of danger and fairly comfortable, Thomas says nothing to worry about. Recovery will take a while but not your concern. Lots of love C & T xx'

Indigo felt relieved. She couldn't believe that she'd dropped off to sleep. Squinting at the time she saw that it was 11 p.m. The sky was clear and the stars twinkled brightly. A half-moon lit up the ocean. Much as she liked her cave, she didn't fancy spending the night there. Half crawling, she made her way up the cliff and staggered home. She really must stop drinking so much. The retreat would help. Tomorrow was a new day and a fresh start.

ELEVEN

Retreat

The morning before the retreat dawned bright and sunny. Indigo had checked the tent and found that it was easy to assemble and had probably never been used. They were expected at the Isle of Mull Healing Centre the following day at lunchtime. She'd spent the previous evening relaxing. She had a hot scented bath, lit a candle and put on some soothing music in the background. Soaking in the tub, she washed her hair, shaving her armpits and legs. She would embrace spirituality and Mother Nature one hundred per cent but that didn't mean to say that she would grow her armpit and leg hair and go make-up free, no way.

She packed a couple of dresses, thick jumpers, wellingtons, socks, leggings, shorts, jeans and t-shirts. Adding a waterproof jacket, blanket, candles and a lantern to the pile, she pondered what else she would need. She had a cold-bag trolley with groceries in it and all her plastic crockery. She added her Kindle, a notepad and pen to the rucksack.

At 9 o'clock she was all set and put her luggage into the campervan. It was a beautiful sunny morning, and she was glad that she'd worn a simple summer dress, cardigan and trainers. Travelling west, she planned to spend the night in the National Park at Loch Lomond. She would board a ferry from Oban to the island the next morning; it would only take about fifty minutes to cross over. The journey was a pleasant one once she had left behind the congestion of the motorways. The roads were lined with dark green forest and dark indigo lochs. Checking her map, she drove down a track signposted with a green area. It was a designated parking area for campervans. Campers were allowed to light fires within the stone circles already set out. Indigo parked in a meadow near the loch, next to a fireplace.

She fancied a swim but the loch was huge and deep unlike the one near William's parents' house. She hadn't heard from him for a week. Although she enjoyed his company and liked him a great deal, upon reflection it was better that she continued with the healing and strengthening process alone. The meltdown she had experienced the night of the storm had taught her that her recovery was in the early stages and although she might feel alright, it didn't take much to push her over the edge. The weather was warm and pleasant and Indigo sat on the camper-van steps soaking up the yellow rays and sipping coffee. Picking up her mobile `phone, she glanced at her text messages. There was one from William.

'Hi English. Been v busy at work, overtime. Hope u enjoy the witches coven. Heal well. Wx'

Indigo tried to ignore the sensation of pleasure that his text brought her. She put on wellingtons and disappeared into the forest to collect wood. When she returned, two other vans had parked a short distance from her. A woman with blonde plats wearing a long hippy-style dress was preparing a fire. Another with brown plats appeared from inside the other van. She wore leggings, boots and a colourful tunic. They were in their mid-fifties. Looking over, they smiled at her, waving. Indigo waved back.

Lighting a fire, she sat eating an omelette that she had pre-pared inside the campervan. One of the women walked across the field to where she sat.

"Hi, I'm Sandy and that's my friend Elaine. We're having a few drinks around the fire later if you fancy joining us."

Indigo smiled.

"Thank you. I'm Indigo. That's nice of you. I don't have any alcohol with me to contribute."

"We have plenty. Elaine makes her own damson wine, free of chemicals. Come over in about an hour if you like."

Indigo took out her meditation mat and sat in front of the fire focusing on the flames. After the grounding exercises she pro-tected herself and carried out Reiki self-healing. Since the storm she had followed this routine every day and also exercised strenuously. She'd also made a conscious effort to reduce her alcohol intake and sleep as much as possible.

Changing into jeans, biker boots and a pink jumper she wandered over to where the women had lit a good strong fire. They'd put out a deck chair for her. Sitting in it, it nearly tipped over. Elaine helped her adjust it. Giggling, Sandy poured out three glasses of damson wine.

"Cheers," they chorused.

"Have you been to Loch Lomond before?" asked Sandy.

"No, passing through really. I'm from East Lothian on my way to Mull and thought it would be relaxing to stop off on the way. Where are you two from?"

"Ireland originally," said Elaine. "We come from the same village."

"We've spent the last ten years travelling," said Sandy.

"After our children got married we decided to leave our husbands and clear off," interjected Elaine.

"The alternative life called us and we answered," announced Sandy happily.

"Good for you." Indigo looked at their contented faces.

"We come here most years," Sandy continued. "We stay as long as we want to... I work as an artist, oils mainly. I spend six months painting land and seascapes and my ex-husband spends the other six months trying to sell them to restaurants, hotels and other touristy places."

"You're still friendly?"

Sandy's brown eyes twinkled.

"I think he was glad to see the back of me. But yes, still friends."

"I worked as a midwife," said Elaine. "If we settle for a while, I still take on the odd six-month contract. I enjoy writing poetry," her blue eyes smiled.

"I'm in transition," said Indigo. She told them that she used to work as a secretary but resigned, discovered Reiki and was on her way to a retreat. They were both intrigued. By glass three their tongues had loosened. Indigo found herself telling them everything that had happened to her over the past year. In return they confessed their secret.

"We're actually together," said Elaine.

"Childhood sweethearts?" commented Indigo.

"I like that. Yes," said Sandy.

"But you prefer to live separately?"

"Well, we're always next door neighbours but yes, we prefer our own living space. It works better."

"We do sleep together quite regularly," said Elaine.

"Indigo doesn't want to know that," Sandy chided.

"Doesn't bother me," Indigo grinned. "You both seem really happy. I think it's nice. Wine's gorgeous."

Elaine looked pleased.

"I've just started selling it to farmers' markets. I put a stanza of one of my poems on the back label of each batch, so people are encouraged to keep buying my wine. The idea is that after ten bottles the poem is complete. They get nice natural wine and I get my poems well known."

"Clever isn't she?" said Sandy.

"Very." Indigo accepted a refill. "This is extremely hospitable of you. I've had a great evening. So relaxing."

"We'll be here next year, same time. Look us up. Do you want to see Sandy's paintings?"

Elaine got to her feet despite Sandy's protests. Having drunk at twice the pace of Indigo, Sandy was struggling to climb out of the deck chair. Elaine and Indigo doubled up with laughter, as her short legs wiggled.

"Oh, stay there old girl." Elaine waved Sandy back down.

She pulled a large canvas from inside the campervan and Indigo found herself looking at the exact forest and loch where they were. The brush strokes were precise, the attention to detail incredible. Indigo stood in awe of such talent.

"That is brilliant. It looks exactly the same, so clever!"

Sandy made another attempt to get up and fell out of the deckchair sideways. She disappeared into the van and came out with a smaller canvas of the same scene.

Taking a pen she wrote on the back of the canvas.

"To Indigo, from one free spirit to another... Sandy Gordon x."

Elaine, not to be outdone, presented her with a bottle of her wine.

"Thank you. Both of you. But I have nothing to give you."

"You can present us with an update of your progress next year. That is the gift we want," hiccupped Elaine.

Indigo said goodnight and goodbye and went back to her van. It was 2 a.m. The women were an inspiration to her. She had made two new friends.

◆ ◆ ◆

Boarding the ferry at Oban, she enjoyed leaning over the side watching the boat unzipping the blue cloth of the ocean. She spotted a dolphin swimming wild and free. It was a thrilling sight. Exhilarated, she marvelled at how good she felt. She was amazed that she'd woken up with a clear head. There was something to be said for home-made natural wine. She would be placing an order when she returned home.

Indigo arrived at the Isle of Mull Healing Centre on time. It was a walled estate with two grand yellow stone pillars, with angels balanced on the top, guarding the entrance. She showed her confirmation of booking form to a stocky middle-aged man and he pulled back the huge black iron gates to let her in. Waving her through, he smiled but said nothing.

The driveway wound through acres of thick lush woodland. A mansion loomed in the distance, built from the same yellow brick as the pillars. The drive forked and she followed the arrows away from the house pointing down another muddy track that led to where the retreat was to be held. It was a serene place. The air was laced with peace and calm. Deeper into the dark damp forest she went. There was a strong smell of foliage. Rays of gold seared through the tree tops like lasers casting pools of lime light as they illuminated the mossy floor. Suddenly, the murky tunnel gave way to an open field that was being used as a car park. Parking the van, Indigo took out her luggage and locked the van.

Weighed down with a tent, sleeping bag and pillow, rucksack and trolley bag, she following the arrows up a steep mud track and over a stile. The view of the bay was spectacular. Acres of farm and woodland stretched all around her. Jumping down the other side, she found herself in a meadow full of long grasses swaying in the wind. The sun was shining and the grass was alive with butterflies of numerous varieties displaying designer wings of blues, browns, reds and yellows. She'd never imagined that there were so many different types.

The grasses were tall, nearly up to her chest in places, but there was a small pathway that she kept to. This ended abruptly at a clearing in the long grass. Indigo was hot and perspiring with exertion. A lavish green field roamed for about two acres, meeting rocks and the sandy beach beyond. A small loch lay to her right surrounded by trees where it connected to the forest on the far side. There were people already putting up tents and constructing fires. A tall grey-haired man of about fifty approached Indigo. He looked fit and healthy, and was smiling as he handed her a leaflet. She was about to say something but he shook his head and put his finger to his lips. He walked away, and she read the leaflet.

'A warm welcome to Isle of Mull Healing Centre Retreat.

'Today, as part of the initial healing process, we will be silent until the gong sounds at 4.30 p.m. This will enable you to adjust to the peaceful setting and begin to cleanse yourself of the stresses of daily life. Please put up your tent, tend to your fire and see to your meal. The loch is safe for swimming but only proficient swimmers should swim out as there are no life guards. The grounds and beach are open for walking and exploration, as are the gardens for meditation. Only the main house is out of bounds.

'When the gong sounds, make your way to the area marked 'campfire' on the map on the reverse of this leaflet. There will be a brief talk and you should dress in loose clothing suitable for light exercise.'

Indigo looked around the field. There were about seven other people there. Some had chosen the pretty location near the loch for their temporary home. It would be nice during the day, but at dusk there would be midges. Others were camping near the woods. Indigo walked down the field past the communal campfire to where the fields met the beach. There was a nice isolated soft spot that overlooked the sea. She had wild grass to the back of her and some rocks to the side to shield her from the wind. Putting up her tent, she placed the cool trolley bag in a hole in the black rocks to the left of her to keep the food cold. Then from her rucksack she took some black bin bags that she'd thought of at the last minute. They were allowed fires but there was no wood provided so she would have to go off to the forest to gather her own. Fortunately she had brought her large flask with her, and so poured herself a cup of tea and ate some cold sausage sandwiches. This was proving to be a fascinating experience already and it had only just begun.

Indigo spent an interesting hour wandering through the woods collecting sticks and larger pieces of wood. Some of the wood was damp but would soon dry out in the sun. She wrapped her wood pile in black sacks placing them by the side of the tent. There was still another hour until the gong sounded. She decided to gather some stones from the beach to construct a fireplace. She tried to choose flat chunky rocks. When her bag was full, she also discovered some old iron that the tide had washed up. It was rusty but would do as a grill to sit her saucepan or frying pan on.

Back at camp, she built the fireplace. It was an oval shape with one side missing and quite sturdy. Filling a saucepan with water, she decided to make a cup of coffee and try it out. She placed some sticks into the fireplace and put a bundle of dried long grass on top. Taking a tea-light from the packet she placed it in the centre and added kindling. She lit the candle and the grass and sticks caught. She presumed that matches were acceptable as nothing had been mentioned about creating fire by rubbing sticks together! Placing the saucepan onto the rusty iron grill, she was impressed when the water began to boil and she filled her coffee mug. The fireplace was an achievement. She sat watching the fire burn.

Changing into leggings and a loose t-shirt, she put on her trainers.

DONG! DONG! DONG!

The gong sounded exactly on time. Tying back her long hair, Indigo made her way to the camp fire area where people were congregating. When they had all arrived, the grey-haired man who had greeted her on arrival came and stood in front of them. He was dressed in jogging bottoms and a grey t-shirt.

"Hi. My name is Gabriel Allen and I run the Isle of Mull Healing Centre retreat. We welcome you here and hope that you find your stay both productive and enjoyable. There are rules and a strict timetable here that some may find difficult but they are necessary. I'll read them out to you, but you will be given a copy:

7.30	We rise by this time. Tea or coffee is permitted but no food until after meditation.
8.00–9.00	Meditation.
9.00	Breakfast.
10.30	Yoga and Reiki.
11.30–4.30	Silence and free time within the grounds. This includes lunchtime.
4.30	Meditation and counselling.
5.30	Dinner.
6.30	Music and communal campfire.
10.00	Latest time to return to tents.

Any questions?"

Indigo looked at her fellow campers. The itinerary sounded good to her.

"So I'm not supposed to talk to anyone for most of the day? How is that going to do me good?" one of the women demanded.

Her tone was aggressive and she looked cross. Indigo could feel bad energy pulsing from her. Her lips were pursed together and she seemed the fault-finding type. Just the sort of negative person that Indigo was desperate to steer clear of.

Gabriel spoke in his deep calm voice.

"Silence is good because it enables you to hear the voice of your higher self. When we talk or listen to others we often miss this important input."

"But breakfast at 9 a.m! My blood sugar is too low."

"Hot chocolate, coffee or tea will help. Meditation works better on an empty stomach, that's all. We wish you to get maximum benefit from your time here."

The woman still looked cross. Perhaps that was her natural expression.

"Now, I will point to each of you and I would like you to tell me your name and a small amount about yourself."

He pointed to the man on Indigo's left. He was small, blond and about thirty with brown eyes and an earnest expression.

"Hi, I'm Ben. I work in IT. I own my own company but I've recently suffered a nervous breakdown. I've managed to hide it

84

from everyone, but I need to fix myself or change, I can't carry on as I was before."

He looked down embarrassed. Indigo smiled at him. It was her turn next.

"Hi, I'm Indigo. I've also had a rough time lately." She could feel the colour rising in her face. "I have denied my spirituality my whole life and now want to do the opposite. It's time for me to be who I'm supposed to be rather than who I think I should be. I want to develop that further. If that makes sense?"

She also looked down for a moment. She hated speaking in front of people. Gabriel nodded. He pointed to the woman on Indigo's right. She was around fifty, small and overweight, with long blonde hair and no make-up.

"My name's Jan, and I'm a florist. I'm married to Keith here next to me. We've had a few problems in our marriage and want to reconcile and find a way forward. We're both very interested in spirituality of all sorts."

Keith was middle-aged, overweight and looked like a bank manager.

"As Jan says, we've had a few problems. We thought this might help. I work in the City of London, a banker. We want to live our lives in a different way to how we have in the past."

The cross woman was next. She was tall, about forty, with dark bobbed hair. She was pretty and looked very athletic.

"My name's Jennifer, and I have studied all aspects of spirituality and healing and wanted to experience a retreat to see if it makes a difference."

"My name is Bernie and I play guitar in a rock band. Bit stressed at the moment and needed some peace." Bernie was about forty-four, with dark hair and a good-looking face. He had bags under his eyes. He had either been working flat out or was on drugs.

"My name's Barbara. My husband and I are getting divorced and I wanted to get away for a while and heal my life." Barbara was about thirty. She looked fit and glamorous, but sad.

"Hi. I'm Robert. I'm thirty-eight and I'm an architect. I've also been feeling the strain of work and wanted a positive experience for myself that doesn't involve pressure." Robert was a serious-looking man, with black hair and blue eyes. He was tall, about six feet.

"Thank you. All of you. These sessions are completely confidential. So anything that is said within the healing group will go no further. Now I need you all to sign the form on the back page acknowledging this."

Gabriel gave everyone a pen. His assistant, a tiny, dark-haired lady, handed around gym mats and collected the signed forms. Next, she and Gabriel disappeared into one of the outbuildings and returned with a giant brass lantern with clear glass. Inside it was a huge candle. They placed it on the ground and lit it. The flame flickered as the casing was closed. Gabriel placed his mat on the ground about two feet from the lantern and instructed everyone to sit in a circle on their mats around the flame. Healing music sounded from the base of the lantern. Gabriel instructed the group to close their eyes and to breathe in deeply, as if filling their whole body with air, and then exhale slowly. This they repeated a number of times. The haunting melody mingled with the sound of waves crashing on the seashore.

Gabriel began to speak:

"You are sitting in a field near the beach, and you are safe. You have walked away and left the stress of daily life behind. Each deep breath that you breathe in heals your mind, body, emotions and soul and each breath exhaled slowly casts negativity and bad feelings out into the universe. There they will disperse and you will be free of them. Now, breathe in to heal your body, exhale slowly to cast out negativity, breathe in to heal your body, exhale slowly to cast out negativity."

They repeated the exercise for about five minutes.

"You have begun the process of healing and have already cast out much of the destructive negative forces that were lurking within each of you. You have done well. Say after me. 'I have done well.'"

"I have done well," chanted the group.

Indigo felt like an idiot, but she knew that to congratulate yourself even for a small achievement was a valuable step forward.

"Now open your eyes. We will go for a short walk and then it will be time for dinner."

They went for a thirty-minute walk along the sandy beach. The sky was now a mass of black rain clouds and the sea was dark grey. The breakers rolling in were huge with angry white tips. Indigo was glad that the tent was new and that she'd packed an extra blanket. The beach was curious with plenty of strange rock formations, pools and thousands of seashells of various shapes and sizes.

Returning to her tent, Indigo put on a thick pink wool jumper with matching socks and a pair of black shorts over her leggings. Putting a woollen hat on her head, she took some wood out of the supplies. She glanced up at the sky and wished that she had collected more. Setting the fire, she pulled on her wellingtons and ventured into the woods to gather more wood. This time she packed the black bin bag full of small and large pieces, and triple bagged it before staggering back to camp.

Placing it next to the other sack, she lit the fire and began cooking the evening meal. Removing the grill, she let the fire burn brightly within the confinement of the fireplace. She cut a cross onto the top of a potato and pushed a lump of butter into the gap. Placing it in tin foil she added salt and pepper. She sealed the foil and dropped it into the fire estimating that it would take about an hour to cook. The campsite fire wasn't obligatory so it wouldn't matter if she was a bit late. Pouring herself some juice, she sat in silence staring into the flames that danced purple, green and orange.

There was a lot of pain within the group and she hoped that they would bond well as this would accelerate the healing pro-cess. Positive energy was what they all needed. Indigo wondered if Jennifer would cause problems. She was an awkward charac-ter, possibly scared and hadn't known what to expect. Some people were defensive or rude when they were nervous, others quiet or standoffish.

The fire calmed to a low flicker and, forking the potato, Indigo took it from the fire. It was soft on the inside. Adding cheese, more butter and salad she enjoyed her second meal camping out in the Scottish outdoors.

The sound of Scottish folk music drifted over from the camp fire area, and the smell of the bonfire reached her nostrils. She took her gym mat and a blanket, and made her way over to the fire. Sitting down at a safe distance, she saw Ben coming over, then Bernie, Jan, Keith, Barbara and Robert. Soon they were all there apart from Jennifer.

"I'm enjoying it so far," said Ben. "Obviously, it takes a while to unwind and adapt. For some, longer than others."

Bernie lit a cigarette.

"Bit uptight that one, ain't she?" He moved his head towards Jennifer's tent.

"Well, we all are in our own way, that's why we're here," Indigo said. Although she hadn't taken to Jennifer either, she didn't want negative vibes or a witch hunt to begin.

"I suppose."

"You're in a band?" Barbara asked Bernie.

"I write music mainly these days. Used to be in a rock band called Strip Tease many years ago. Doubt anyone's heard of it."

He offered Barbara his cigarette and she inhaled deeply. Indigo felt a bit indignant. To get stoned or high using drugs couldn't be the right way to access the spiritual path. It was using false means to get to a fabricated state. Natural channelling through the higher self had to be the way. Jan looked equally perturbed when Barbara offered it to her.

"No thank you." She glanced at her husband Keith as if to gauge his reaction. To Indigo's surprise he took the marijuana joint and inhaled deeply.

Indigo glanced at Jan who swore at her husband and stormed back to their tent. Indigo sighed. She wished she'd signed up to go on a retreat on her own. In truth, she couldn't be bothered with other people's issues. She wasn't interested and didn't have the energy to cope with them. She didn't want to leave in a worse state than when she'd arrived.

Ben and Robert exchanged glances.

"Indigo?" Keith offered her the joint.

"No thanks, I don't do drugs."

"You don't mind if we do?" Keith seemed concerned.

"Your wife seemed to object..."

"Oh, don't mind her. She doesn't know how to have fun."

"This is a place of healing," said Robert in his matter-of-fact way.

"Did you want to come here, Keith?" asked Indigo, as it was obvious that he hadn't.

"Came to please the wife."

"I came out of desperation," said Ben pointedly. "I sat there one day at the kitchen table with a bottle of scotch and a packet of paracetamol and tossed a coin. Live or die. It landed on live. I cried because I'd have to find the strength and courage to carry on. The next day, surfing the Internet, clicking here and there, I discovered this place."

"My story is similar," said Robert. "I came here to heal my life. I've become a workaholic and my marriage is in tatters. I have to find another way to live or I'll die. Maybe not physically, but spiritually."

"I'm a drunk," blurted out Barbara. "My husband wore himself out trying to help me, but in the end he couldn't stand being near me any longer. I sucked the life out of him. I hope that if I heal then he'll stop the divorce."

"And your wife loves you so much, that she dragged you here. That's her desperate story," Indigo said to Keith.

"Sometimes more effort is needed, and we have to learn to be less selfish, more considerate," said Barbara. She looked a bit stoned. Bernie was rolling another joint.

Keith nodded.

"I apologise. Guess I've got a lot to learn too."

"We all have," said Indigo.

She said goodnight to the group and returned to her tent early. It had been a weird evening, but the chat around the bonfire had bonded the group. Indigo stood outside looking up at the sky while she cleaned her teeth. Droplets of rain began to fall becoming bigger and faster. The fire was dead and so Indigo replaced the grill and covered the fireplace with bin bags and rocks.

Lighting a lantern, she crawled into the tent and zipped it up watertight. The rainfall became torrential, hammering onto the canvas roof. The music stopped abruptly and she could hear shrieks as the group around the campfire raced back to their tents. It had been good to acquaint herself with the others, but on a spiritual healing retreat the conversation was never going to be the same as if she'd met them at a caravan park or holiday camp.

The tent had a baptism of water on its first night, as the rain was relentless. Indigo was worried at one point that she would get washed out to sea. She wondered if the tent would float. Her perfect camping spot was picturesque but wouldn't be practical if the rain continued to fall. Around four o'clock, light began to penetrate the tent and Indigo finally fell asleep.

TWELVE

Casting Out

Feeling around for her alarm, Indigo bashed her ˋphone trying to stop it from bleeping. She'd only just dropped off to sleep. Rubbing her eyes she tried to focus on the time: it read 7.00 a.m. She had an hour until meditation. Poking her head out of the tent, she saw whiteness. The campsite was shrouded in mist from the sea. The rainfall had ceased. The thought of dipping herself half-naked into the loch was less appealing early in the morning with a chill in the air. But Indigo was determined to embrace the experience. Resetting and lighting the fire, she put on her dressing gown and wellingtons and went to the loch. The water was clear with a sandy base. The forest cupped the far side of the water and she could see birds flying from the loch back up high into the trees.

Looking around she saw that the site was deserted. Stripping down to her bikini that she'd brought for this purpose, she plunged into the icy water. Gasping as the cold hit her warm body it took a moment for her to catch her breath. She swam for a while before duck-diving down into the depths to wet her hair. She wasn't sure if they were allowed to use shampoo but she did anyway. She swam out to about half-way hoping that there weren't any fish or creatures gazing longingly at her naked toes. Feeling like a mermaid she swam underwater back to the shore. Emerging from the water shaking and shivering with cold she felt a primitive satisfaction. She wrapped herself in a bath towel and hurried back to the tent.

After three cups of tea in front of the fire, she put on make-up using a hand mirror and dressed in the clothes she had worn the previous evening. Gabriel had lit the campfire as the morning was cold and crisp. He must also have a supply of dry wood. They sat in a circle around the lantern on their large waterproof mats. All were present. Barbara and Bernie looked rough, and there was an atmosphere between the married couple Jan and Keith. The healing music began and upon Gabriel's command they closed their eyes and followed the breathing exercises for five minutes as they had the day before.

"You have breathed in the pure healing energy supplied by Mother Earth and you have cast out bad energy. All aspects of negativity have been sent out into the universe. You are safe and surrounded by nature, peace and love. Repeat after me:

"To all those who have done me wrong, I forgive you."

The group chanted the response.

"Think of someone who had done wrong to you. Take the feeling and cast it out to the universe, saying 'I forgive you'."

"I forgive you," repeated the group.

"You are free of stress. Wander amongst nature and ask your higher self to guide the way forward. Meditate and listen to your inner voice. You are wandering through fields of long grasses, surrounded by flowers of mauve, yellow and blue. Birds, bees and butterflies move about their daily work, all is calm. The sound of the sea can be heard in the distance, a source of pure energy that is connected to the higher power. Sit near the source and soak in the waves of energy. Now, open your eyes..."

Gabriel smiled. His assistant handed around paper pads and pens.

"Today at free time, find a peaceful spot. Sit on your own and write on the pad who has hurt you and why. No-one will read it, so you can put every thought and emotion down on paper. Then write at the bottom: 'I forgive you and cast you out to the universe'. You can fill up several notepads if you wish. Lana has more and you can write about as many people or experiences as you want. Bring them here at meditation time and you will burn them in the fire. The negativity will be cast out to the universe and disperse. It is unhealthy to keep bad feelings within as it can manifest into physical and mental illness and cause you to leak energy."

He clapped his hands together.

"Now, go and enjoy breakfast. We will return here at 10.30 for yoga outside and Reiki over there in the Reiki hut." He pointed to the outbuilding that looked like a log cabin situated near to the loch.

Indigo walked back to the tent and put more wood on the fire. Gabriel had a great job, she thought. How nice it would be to live in peace amongst nature, removed from the chaotic madness of the outside world. Taking eggs and quorn deli-rashers from the cold bag, she fried veggie bacon and eggs, managing to balance the saucepan of water on the rusty grill at the same time for her tea. She was really impressed by her fireplace. The food tasted delicious. She wondered for a moment how the others were getting on, but threw out the thought. It was not her concern. After breakfast she washed the dishes in the loch, and returned to her tent for a power nap. She awoke abruptly as the gong sounded for yoga and Reiki.

Indigo lay with her leg up in the air, listening to the soothing trance music. It was her turn next for Reiki. Upon arrival at yoga they had each taken a crystal number from the smooth cut-glass bowl. Hers had been number five. Idly she watched Jennifer practising yoga. She put maximum effort into everything but her face was set in a tight mask. It was as if she was going through the motions but did not understand it. Jennifer looked over at her and Indigo smiled. Jennifer glared back and looked away. But Indigo felt energised, happy and alive. She felt sorry for Jennifer who was all knotted up inside. Perhaps Reiki would help her.

The log cabin looked out across the loch. The sun came out casting a golden pathway across the water to the leafy forest beyond. The room was warm and smelled of fresh wood and lavender with a trace of burning logs from the small log burner. Gabriel took her hands and smiled into her eyes.

She lay down on the white couch. Shutting her eyes she enjoyed the waves of heat and power that coursed through her. The colours seemed more vivid than usual, emerald, gold, deep rich purple and scarlet. A feeling of warmth and peace encompassed her and again she had an image of hills, lochs and a figure who exuded strength. Gabriel moved away and she lay there for a while enjoying the feeling of total relaxation. A small bell sounded and she sat up.

"How are you feeling?" he asked. He was standing watching her.

"Really good."

"You have very high good energy," he placed his hand on her head, "despite all that you have been through." He nodded. "Some of which no-one knows about. Your energy flows well. You have a small flame of faith that burns brighter with every positive breath you take. You should be proud of what you've achieved."

"Are you psychic?"

He chuckled. His blue eyes twinkled.

"I'm tuned into my higher self and the higher powers..."

"Thank you Gabriel," said Indigo. He shook her hand.

"Enjoy your free time. From the moment you walk out of here it is silence until 4.30. Remember the exercise set earlier."

Indigo packed a water bottle, sandwiches, a flask of tea and the note pad into her small rucksack. Dressing in jeans, t-shirt and wellingtons, she tied a jumper around her waist. The sky was cloudy and so she added a waterproof jacket.

She decided to begin her exploration of the grounds by visiting the forest, then moving to the peace garden and then on to the beach. She would find a rock and write the negative energy exercise there. Just as she was walking to the edge of the forest, Jennifer came striding up to her.

"Are you going for a walk? Not sure it's up to par here. Nothing like the retreats I've read about and that Gabriel guy's really weird and I'm sure Bernie's some sort of drug addict. I'll come along with you." She lit a cigarette.

Indigo looked at her and shook her head. She was surprised by the approach. Indigo had believed initially that Jennifer was suffering from some kind of inner pain which would explain her obnoxious attitude, but now she realised that she simply wasn't a nice person. She didn't want to alienate her by being unfriendly, but at the same time she couldn't break the vow of silence, besides they were supposed to walk alone.

Jennifer was waiting for a response.

"Oh, you're not following that stupid silence thing are you? Oh ok, I'll talk then and you can listen."

Indigo felt horrified at the prospect of her precious afternoon being shattered by this awful woman droning on. She put her hands up, shook her head and walked off. Jennifer was negative and a leech that would suck out her positive energy. Indigo was still too fragile to be around someone like that. It bothered her for a moment that she was still attracting that type of person. Then she considered that she had said 'no' and walked away. A month ago, she would have reluctantly let Jennifer come along and wreck the afternoon. She was making progress. Additionally, she had recognised Jennifer as a negative sucker, and that was another breakthrough.

The temperature had risen since the morning and the sun was shining through the trees. The woods were dark and dank containing trees with strange twisted trunks. They were perfect for holding a tree house. Moss and weeds grew up through the cracks in the fallen trees and a multitude of pathways gave a selection of walks. The sea was to Indigo's left and she veered to the right. Suddenly she began to feel anxious and worried; Jeremy Clifford-Amos and Mike came into her mind and the feeling of flat dread increased. She looked up at the tree tops. Why was this place making her feel like that? Jennifer's face flashed in front of her eyes, these negative feelings had been caused by her and her bad energy. Surely, Indigo was stronger than her? This revelation helped Indigo realise how vulnerable she still was. She would counteract the negativity in the garden of peace.

Walking down a cobbled path she came to an oak door that led to the walled garden. Taking the black iron ring in her hand she opened the door and walked in. The walls were covered by climbing roses of pink and white. The flower beds below lined the walls and were packed full of dark orange poppies. In the middle was an ornate pond full of fish surrounded by yellow and blue flowers.

At intervals set against the wall between the flowers, dark green shrubs, cut into the shape of angels with great wings, framed six pools of water. These pools were like small lagoons suitable for bathing. The angels sheltered the swimmer from prying eyes. A small waterfall cascaded down a rockery into the water below. A prayer mat sat to the side of the pool and a small version of the clear brass lantern was held in the palm of a white angel statue. Indigo walked to the pool at the end of the garden as it looked especially secluded. Squeezing through a small gap in the angels' wings she lit the candle and sat on the mat. Only the sound of birds chirping could be heard. The day had become warm and she removed her wellingtons and socks and dipped her toe into the water. To her surprise it was like a hot bath. Indigo stood up and looked down the length of the garden. The other pools appeared unoccupied.

Stripping off her clothes she submerged herself naked into the gentle warmth of the mini lagoon. The sun cast luminous rays through the wings and as she floated she could see the brilliant colours of the flowers through gaps in the hedgerows. Her mind drifted to the Reiki experienced that morning. She was sure that nature and meditation had enhanced the experience. The flat, anxious feeling left her and as she luxuriated in the pool she felt strong again.

After a couple of hours she reluctantly left the garden of peace and made her way back to the forest. The trees were welcoming this time and she enjoyed the sound of the mysterious rustling woodland.

Later, clambering over a pile of rocks, Indigo came to a small cove that contained a small rock formation resembling a throne. The tide was out and the sea was a greyish blue.

"Perfect!"

Taking out her flask and cheese and pickle sandwich, she ate a late lunch before embarking on the negative energy task. She didn't feel inclined to do the task for she was loathe to return to the past and dig up bad feelings. Negativity was lurking in the depths of her being however and had to be eliminated. She decided to add Jennifer to the ever-growing list.

An hour later she had written in length and detail about Mike and her true feelings in every sense, about Jeremy Clifford-Amos, her ex-husband who had been physically abusive, and an old friend of hers who had caused her anguish shortly after her divorce. She added Jennifer at the end, because she had annoyed her. The paper was almost vibrating with negativity and Indigo half expected it to combust.

The 4.30 gong sounded and she made her way to the campfire. All of the others were there already and waved and smiled at her. Jennifer ignored her.

Gabriel was standing there looking cheerful. The campfire was blazing and the mats were in position around the giant lantern. The healing music was playing in the background.

"We've been blessed with another glorious afternoon," he said enthusiastically. "Has everyone managed to complete the task?"

The group murmured affirmatively. Indigo noticed that the pieces of paper they held varied in size. Hers was thick and so was Ben's, Robert's and, surprisingly, Keith's. Not that the quantity mattered, it was the content that counted.

"Who would like to go first?" asked Gabriel.

Indigo's hand shot up. She couldn't wait to get rid of the bundle of paper before it came back and contaminated her.

"Indigo, place it into the fire and say 'I cast all negativity, bad memories and emotions into the fire and out to the universe where they will disperse and never affect me again.'"

Indigo stepped forward. She could feel the intense heat of the fire against her face. Finding a gap in the wood she thrust the papers forward, dropping them into the fire.

"I cast all negativity, bad memories and emotions into the fire and out to the universe where they will disperse and never affect me again," she said firmly, feeling a lightening within.

Each member of the group burned their paper. Jennifer looked mutinous when it was her turn. Afterwards they sat down on their mats and did the breathing exercise.

"You have cast your negativity into the fire and out to the universe. It can never visit you again. You have freed your whole being from a dark force. You have experienced Reiki and yoga and all chakras have been freed of blockages so that your energy may flow. You have done well. Now you are at peace, and are free to tune into your higher self without obstruction. Now relax and let the beauty of nature soak into your souls and allow the music to wash over you."

They sat for ten minutes in silent meditation.

"Now open your eyes," said Gabriel. "Is there anything that anyone would like to discuss, either as a group or in private?"

The married couple raised their hands and requested a private counselling session, and so did Jennifer. The other members of the group seemed content.

"Ok. Jan, Keith and Jennifer. If you would like to continue meditation until I call each of you. The rest of you may leave. There will be dancing, music and light refreshments here tonight."

Indigo smiled at the others and disappeared back to her end of the field. It had been a wonderful day, but she felt tired and needed to sleep for a couple of hours. Setting the alarm on her `phone, she crawled into the tent and fell asleep.

THIRTEEN

At One

When she awoke it was six o'clock in the evening. Sipping tea, she stretched while waiting for her can of lentil soup to heat up. She could see in the distance that Gabriel was in discussion with Jennifer. Her stance was aggressive and he moved away from her. Then, she bent down and began packing up her tent. Jan stood nearby looking upset. Indigo was about to join them, but stopped herself. That was her old self. She wouldn't get involved. She was not responsible for Jennifer or her life. It was Jennifer's personal journey and if she chose to sabotage it, then that was her affair.

Her soup tasted nice, it was thick and satisfying. By the time she went to wash up the dishes in the loch, Jennifer had gone and Gabriel was tending to the fire. He disappeared into the Reiki hut, perhaps to ask for divine strength.

The music started at six-thirty, a mix of dance and folk music with a few gypsy strums thrown in. Picnic tables had been placed near the fire loaded with lemonade, orange juice, white and red grape juice, jugs of water, fruit, cheese and crisps. It was a mild evening and the sky was a clear light blue. When the group congregated, Gabriel and Lana emerged from the Reiki hut.

Gabriel addressed the group.

"Good evening to you all. I see that the energy is good and you all appear rested. Jennifer has decided to leave us. The healing retreat is not for everyone and this happens from time to time."

Everyone looked at each other.

"She was an uptight cow that one," said Bernie. "Good riddance to her I say. I'm 'aving a smashing time."

"All of our energies and desires are unique, Bernie," Gabriel smiled and waved at the refreshments. "I am very pleased with the progress that you're all making and I hope that you are too. Enjoy!"

"May I get you a drink, Indigo?" asked Robert.

"A large red grape juice, please." Indigo was desperate for a glass of wine, but she would have to pretend that the grape juice was alcoholic. He returned with drinks and they sat at one of the picnic benches. Jan came over. She looked much happier.

"Are you finding the retreat a good experience?" asked Indigo.

"Yes", she said, "I'm sorry about my language last night. Keith, he didn't really want to come. Said it was a bunch of hippy nonsense, and he kept making fun of everything. He even smoked that marijuana yesterday to wind me up." She took a sip of white grape juice. "When he came back to the tent last night, he apologised. I thought he was stoned, and so we had a row this morning early. But he's adamant that he genuinely wants to dig deep and discover his true self and make our marriage work. He even told Gabriel. I don't know if something happened last night after I left but it's like a miracle. He's been a closed book ever since I've known him."

"That's fantastic," Robert squeezed her hand. "That's great progress, and credit to you for sticking by him. Ben looks happier too."

They looked over at Ben who was in deep conversation with Gabriel and Keith.

"And those two seem to be getting on well," said Indigo, referring to Barbara and Bernie who were lying on a mat near the fire giggling like a couple of teenagers.

"I think they may be soul-mates," grinned Robert.

"How about you, Robert?"

"I've got my perspective back. I have discovered how to meditate, practise yoga and I've experienced Reiki. I now know how to manage stress and my life. How to get and maintain the balance that I need, and so has Ben, that's why he looks so happy. I've found a new best mate in him. We've already had some great conversations. We'll support each other from now on." He took a swig of lemonade. "You can't put a price on friendship, knowledge and positive experiences."

"I agree," said Indigo.

They chatted until about 9 o'clock and then Lana began to dance around the campfire. The group found this amusing.

"Come on. Join in. Dump your inhibitions," shouted Keith, and began dancing wildly around the fire. Jan looked at him incredulously and burst out laughing. She looked up at the sky.

"Do you think Keith has been abducted by aliens and this wonderful creature put here in his place?"

"If he has then you've got the better deal," laughed Indigo.

Jan went to join him and soon all the others apart from Bernie and Barbara joined in. Indigo felt stupid to begin with but then began to enjoy herself.

The gong sounded at ten and they all retired for the night. Bernie and Barbara had already disappeared.

◆ ◆ ◆

The next morning Indigo followed her routine. She felt much more alert after a good night's sleep and, lighting the fire, set off to the loch with her towel. This time she tied her hair in a bun and swam over to the other shore near the forest. It was invigorating swimming in the freezing deep water and she swam strongly for about twenty minutes.

Shivering, she sprinted back to the tent and dressed quickly. After three cups of tea it was time for meditation. The fire was lit, for the day was sunny but cool. The sky was blue with a smattering of clouds and there was a light breeze. Indigo waved at the rest of the group and took her place on the meditation mat. The lantern was lit and the healing music filled the camp. They repeated the breathing exercises.

"You have eradicated negativity and freed your chakras from blockages. You are safe and your energy is flowing well. Today you must listen to your positive thoughts and the voice of your higher self. If you have any negative thoughts, cast them out and change them to positive ones. Enjoy your free time. Float in the hot lagoons in the peace garden or trek through the dark green leafy forest; or peruse the beach exploring the caves and rock pools, but listen to your higher self." Gabriel finished speaking.

They sat in silent meditation for ten minutes.

"Now you may open your eyes... see you back here at 10.30."

Indigo cooked herself a cheese omelette for breakfast and had a cup of coffee. Washing up the dishes she tidied the inside of the tent. They would be leaving shortly after the afternoon's meditation. She wished that she could stay longer. The estate was beautiful and there were so many different places to explore.

Rolling back onto her shoulders, Indigo rested her knees onto her face. She then moved her legs straight up into the air in a shoulder stand. Yoga was something she would take up when she got home. She was fairly fit but not as flexible as she would like to be. After yoga she returned to the tent. She had declined Reiki because she wanted to practise self-healing sitting either on the beach or in the peace garden.

A number of the group were heading in the direction of the peace garden. They hadn't realised that the hot tub lagoons existed until Gabriel mentioned them at meditation, so Indigo decided to go to the beach. The sea was a source of high energy and it would be an interesting exercise. Indigo dressed in leggings, shorts, t-shirt and a thick jumper; adding wellingtons, she picked up a water bottle and waterproof mat and set off.

Crunching over black, grey and white stones, hundreds of shells and strands of slimy lime seaweed, she made her way to the far end of the beach. The tide was on the turn and the sun glowed through hazy cloud. The sea was a deep blue. Reaching the small cove sheltered from the wind by black boulders, she placed the waterproof mat on a clean stretch of soft yellow sand.

Sitting on the mat she pressed her palms together and closed her eyes concentrating on the sound of the breakers smashing onto the sea shore. Opening her eyes she continued to focus, absorbing the sight of the ocean. Then she called Reiki for herself. Placing her hands in the correct positions she carried out self-healing, to clear and heal her chakras. Indigo asked to be healed of negativity, bad health and to be blessed with mental clarity, confidence and intuition.

The energy flowed through her. Opening her eyes, the scene before her was illuminated. The sound of the tide and wildlife magnified. The blue of the sea was brilliant sapphire, the green hills bright emerald, the fields full of wild grasses a vibrant mass of rich colour. Her senses were heightened and her mind felt alert. A powerful energy vibrated around her. A feeling of peace and strength filled her.

Indigo felt powerful, confident and loved. The warmth was incredible. She sat there enjoying the energy waves circling her. Holding up her hands she could see a light blue shadow around them and a thick line of light blue energy flowing between her palms. Ending the session, she thanked Jesus, the angels and the universe for the gift that she'd been given. She felt privileged.

FOURTEEN

A New Life

T urning into Wallace Cuthbert's drive, Indigo reflected that the weekend had been one of the best of her life. She had exchanged mobile numbers with the entire group including Gabriel. The retreat had been a valuable experience and they planned to meet again at the next one. It was still early days for all members of the group, but she felt that open wounds had healed over the weekend.

Before leaving, Indigo expressed an interest in Gabriel's work. He responded by offering to teach her everything he knew. His support made her feel secure. She had listened to her higher self and the way forward was clear.

The lawns were perfectly cut, with precise edges. No dry or bald patches could be seen. Red roses were perched along the boundaries, swaying in the wind. Their beds were full of rich soil. There was not a weed in sight. William had been busy.

Wallace's car was absent from the drive and Indigo stuffed her dirty laundry into the washing machine and went upstairs to run a bath. Soaking in the rose-scented water, she closed her eyes and dozed. After washing her hair, shaving her legs and underarms, she was rinsing herself in the shower when she heard a banging on the bedroom door. She wrapped herself in a towel and walked into the bedroom as William opened the door.

"Oh good, you're back! Wallace slipped over on the golf course. He's hurt his back and leg. The doctor's seen to him, it's just a pull but he's in pain. I've got to get back to work. Can you help?"

"Of course."

Indigo rushed into the dressing room and pulled on a summer dress before following William downstairs. Despite the warm evening he had on his police jumper and jacket. Wallace was lying on his bed fully clothed, looking ashen.

"Sorry to be such a bother," he said feebly, "damn slippery mud, or bunny hole or something. Just landed awkwardly."

"No bother," said Indigo and William in unison.

"I'll make some tea," said Indigo, as William helped him into his night clothes.

"Coffee, Imogen, please and a large brandy to go with it," Wallace called after her.

Indigo smiled. She would always be Imogen to Wallace, there was no point correcting him. She returned with a tray laden with coffee, a bottle of brandy, a crystal glass and some chocolate chip cookies.

"I made you a coffee too, William."

He smiled at her, although she could tell from his eyes that his mind had already returned to work.

"Thanks." He sat on the bed and took Wallace's hand. "You're ok?"

"Aye."

"You've had painkillers, and Indigo will give you more in two hours. If it gets any worse you're to tell her. Muscle spasms or anything like that. Do you want the telly on?"

"Aye." Wallace drained the glass of brandy and laid his head back on the pillow. He looked tired.

"There, I've put the snooker on for you." He handed Wallace the remote control. "I'll be back after my shift around ten."

He took the tray out and closed the bedroom door behind them.

"He'll be ok, just a bit sore. If it wasn't for the old war wound he'd probably have got up and carried on playing." He handed her the tray. "Can you check on him every hour? See you later." He walked towards the door. Turning, he called: "Indigo, did you have a good weekend?"

"Yes, it was fantastic."

"You're looking well on it."

He sped off in the police car.

Indigo checked Wallace after an hour. He was sleeping and his breathing was easy and regular. Chopping onions, broccoli, potato and carrots, she fried the onions before throwing in the other ingredients with water plus two stock cubes. When it was cooked she liquidised the mixture and added salt, pepper and stilton. That would do for Wallace's tea, and William could have some too. She put a bowl of soup onto a tray with salt, pepper, bread and a cup of coffee, and headed back to his room.

He was awake and had eased himself into a sitting position.

"You're an angel," he said, eyeing the dinner tray, "just what my stomach ordered."

Indigo handed him some painkillers and a glass of water.

He asked her about her weekend away. He was very interested in the Isle of Mull Healing Centre retreat, especially Reiki.

"You can experiment on me if you wish after dinner."

"Ok! I'm a beginner but it still works. I'm allowed to treat friends and family."

"I would like to try Reiki," he said. "I have always been a believer and had faith in another power. God knows, being a member of the armed forces my faith was tested enough times. Ruby, my wife, she didn't believe in anything. Especially monogamy." He chuckled and grimaced as his back reminded him of the fall. "Quite beautiful and charming she was, but pointless and empty. I remember thinking after we were married that marrying Ruby was a bit like giving a child a beautiful ornate box for Christmas. When they opened it there was nothing in it... what was the point of it? Yes, that was Ruby. Looks are important, yes, but coupled with substance. A woman of substance, you can't beat."

"So she had affairs, and you tried to make it work?"

"I tried to make the marriage work, and she had affairs with other men. Nothing any man could do would have been enough for that woman." He echoed William's words. "One didn't really divorce in those days, and I thought I'm buggered if I'm going to live in misery without sex for the rest of my days, paying for the harlot. So I offered her an allowance and the safe mask of marriage. She could carry on as she pleased. She accepted and I started an affair with Paula from the village bakery in Direlton. We fell in love and are still together."

"Good," said Indigo, patting his hand. "It would have been such a waste if you'd been left on your own unhappy."

"What about you?"

Indigo poured them both a brandy and told him about her marriage, children and two ex-partners.

"Don't leave it too long, Imogen," said Wallace. "You deserve happiness too."

"No, I won't. I just have other priorities at the moment."

"Those moments slip into hours, days and weeks. Before you know it years have passed and you'll be old like me!" He took a sip of brandy. "People like you deserve to find happiness and a good partner who is worthy of you."

"Thank you."

She picked up his tray and turned to take it out to the kitchen. William was standing in the shadows of the doorway and she jumped. He moved out of the way as she approached, and entered the room. Returning, she saw that he had put the side lamp on and drawn the curtains. He was chatting to Wallace about his day.

"Wallace tells me that you're going to do some Reiki on him."

"Yes," said Indigo.

"May I use Indigo's bathroom to take a shower?" he asked both of them.

Indigo nodded.

"Of course," Wallace said, "but there are plenty of guest bathrooms."

"Save messing one of them up," he said.

Indigo got him a towel out of the airing cupboard.

"There's some soup in the kitchen, William, if you're hungry."

"Thanks."

Indigo fetched her Reiki tools of lavender, candles and iPod.

Lighting candles, she put some lavender on to a black silk scarf and turned off Wallace's side lamp. Reiki healing music drifted from her iPod placed in Wallace's docking station. It was probably the first time that it had been used. She called Reiki for him and placed her hands under his lower skull. Then she moved to the crown chakra and slowly applied Reiki to each chakra. When she had finished, she paid special attention to his leg and back area where he had fallen that day, and to the area of the war wound. She spent time concentrating on healing all wounds, old and new. She thanked the higher powers and ended the session.

"You may open your eyes now," she said.

Wallace opened his eyes.

"That was relaxing. I could feel a lot of heat coming from your hands."

"That's the healing power, the Reiki. You may need more than one session. Six is the average that is recommended."

"Have you finished your witchery?" William walked in with a cup of cocoa. His hair was wet from the shower and he smelled of apple soap. Indigo grinned and collected up her Reiki tools.

"May we use the lounge?" he asked Wallace. "I'd like to stay over on the sofa, Wallace, if that's ok. It's my day off tomorrow."

Wallace looked pleased.

"You can use a bedroom."

"Sofa'll be fine, thanks though."

"I'd like that. Good of you to stay, thank you, William. Light a fire. There's a cold wind tonight."

"Indigo, you'll join me for a couple of drinks? My days off are few and far between."

Both men looked at her expectantly.

"Yes, of course."

"I just need a few minutes to see to this gentleman," said William.

Indigo went upstairs. She looked good. William was right, the retreat had been beneficial. Changing into pyjamas similar to fleecy leggings and a t-shirt, she put on thick woollen socks and made her way to the lounge. There was a chill in the air so Indigo lit the wood burner and lots of candles to make the room relaxing and light. Leaving the doors to the fire open she watched the orange and purple flames dancing in the grate.

William came in with two glasses and a bottle of red wine. He sat down on the sofa next to her. His green eyes glittered in the firelight. He was dressed in gym clothes and thick socks.

"These are the only civilian clothes I had in the car," he said.

"You have a good relationship with Wallace."

"Aye, he's been like an uncle to me. My dad and he are good friends. They met at sixteen, served together in the navy and married similar women. I guess that builds quite a bond. My dad's a good father and Wallace has been great too. I do what I can for him, because I want to."

He looked at Indigo in a challenging manner.

"No, I think that's great. What's your mum like?"

"Like Ruby, but a bit sweeter. She loves me, just couldn't be bothered with motherhood. It interfered with her social calendar and her men friends. She and Dad are still married. She drinks now and he's been having an affair with a woman from the WI for years. He actually met her through Mum. He thinks no-one knows but Wallace and I do."

"Are you married, William?"

William was silent for a while. He sat looking into the fire before re-filling their glasses. He drank half of his before answering.

"I was. Unfortunately she was yet another Ruby. I was trying to build a home and career to bring money in and she was shagging her way through my friends and half of Scotland. Three of my best friends, who had declined her out of loyalty to me, took me to the pub one night, sat me down and told me. I was horrified. I'd been preoccupied working but I'd made a point of communicating with her all the time and telling her what I was doing and why. I was affectionate, I expressed emotion. And I wasn't lacking in the bedroom."

He drained his glass.

"I sat and listened to my friends and nodded. This feeling started in the pit of my stomach and spread through me, a dark foulness. I went home and asked her outright. She confessed and ripped my character to shreds, calling me every name under the sun and then started on my parents and Wallace. Then she hit me in the face and started kicking and punching me. I slapped her really hard, her cheekbone went purple and she called the police."

He looked Indigo straight in the eyes.

"I've never hit a woman before and I swear I haven't since. I don't believe in it. I meet wife-beaters all the time in my job and loathe them. She went too far. She said vile things that were disgusting and untrue. I told my sergeant about it, but no-one else. The police logged it as 'a domestic'. It was a black mark on my record. I knew it could never happen again and so I left her."

"Do you have any children?"

"We have a son, Jack. I brought him up and he visited her every other weekend. He went to Aberdeen Uni studying Physics, got his degree and is travelling in New Zealand for a year before he does his Masters. He's twenty-four. Where are your two?"

"They're staying at their dad's in France for three weeks.

They'll travel from there to their grandparents in Italy for a fortnight before returning to Scotland. The plan was for them to stay with me for a couple of weeks before going back to Leeds."

He nodded.

"I'm not a monster, Indigo."

He refilled their glasses and went to get another bottle.

"I didn't think that you were, William, not for a minute," she said when he returned. "I'm not a violent person either but I slapped my ex-husband once."

"Hmm, that's different."

"Why?"

"Because he was abusive."

"So was she. Just in a different way." Indigo took a sip of wine. "You can't let your past define your future, you know that, William."

"I do. I haven't. I just wanted to be honest with you. I thought you might hate me for it."

"I don't, it wasn't your fault. You were listening at the door, weren't you?"

"I'd just walked in the front door and was about to come in the room. I'd be a pretty crap policeman if I wasn't curious. I learnt a wealth of information about you, Indigo, in a matter of minutes, and a few things about Wallace too. I think what you've achieved in such a short space of time is great. You're a woman of substance, that's for sure." He stood up and stretched. "I'm going to make sure the old man's cleaned his teeth and get him a night cap. Then we'll have a dance to some music. It won't disturb Wallace. These walls are thick and the lounge is far from his bedroom."

A few minutes later, William returned and soon the room was filled with gentle rock music. Pulling Indigo up from the sofa he pressed her to his chest. She could feel his hard muscles against her body. Bending over, he rested his ear against the side of her head and they swayed back and forth to the rhythm. There was strong sexual chemistry between them, but Indigo had learned from her experience with Mike that it was better to concentrate on the spiritual side of a friendship rather than the physical.

She had known William for a short time, but he already trusted her. They knew about each other's pasts, the bleak times when they were both vulnerable. Neither of them was perfect, but that didn't matter because they were friends, and their feelings towards each other were unconditional. Indigo didn't want a relationship where someone tried to own her or dictate to her. She wanted to build a trusting friendship that would allow freedom.

William twirled her around.

"One for the road."

Indigo was tipsy but enjoying herself. She sank back down onto the sofa, smiling at him.

"So what's next for you, Indigo?"

"I'm going to practise Reiki when I've completed my Reiki level two, then become a Reiki Master. Wallace has an old out-building that he converted into a studio years ago which would be ideal for a Reiki healing clinic. I'm going to ask him if I can hire it. I'll complete the Reiki training in Canterbury with Rebecca. Gabriel wants to be my mentor, and I may run retreats too." She took a sip of wine. "For now, I want to spend some time healing and having good positive experiences. I'm looking forward to seeing the children at the end of August. We're very close. Wallace is happy for them to stay here for a couple of weeks. Obviously I'll pay him extra, under protest no doubt. What about you, William?"

"I'm happy with everything I have in my life right now."

The fire crackled and hissed in the grate. The music played softly in the background. William took her hand and leaned his head on the side of the sofa. His eyes closed and Indigo sat for a while watching him in the safety of sleep. Extracting herself, she put his legs up onto the sofa and covered him over with a blanket. Shutting the wood burner doors, she left a lantern lit and went to bed.

"All I have is now," she murmured to herself before she fell asleep. All was well in her world.

◆ ◆ ◆

She was lying on long, flattened emerald grass under an apple tree. The tree was grey with ancient gnarled bark. Roses of red, yellow and cream grew in disarray and a heady perfume wafted around her. Bluebells and white snowdrops grew in clusters around the bases of numerous leafy trees laden with ripe plump fruits. Golden butterflies with amethyst spots glittered as they fluttered past. Composers of nature's symphonies blew their sweet bird song into the mild breeze. The sun warmed her naked body as it blazed through thick branches boasting dark green leaves and bunches of fat, juicy red apples.

A river shining like clear glass raced through the countryside gurgling over boulders, forming a white frothing waterfall. The dark blue sky was cloud-free. Indigo stretched, luxuriating in the atmosphere of peace and contentment. A figure moved to her left. She sat up. She was at one with nature and it didn't matter that she was naked. A man with long hair, dressed in cream muslin robes was standing by the water's edge. She had seen him before in her dreams. His piercing blue eyes were smiling into hers. Raising his left hand high above his head, a brilliant source of white light poured from his palm streaming into her crown. Power, warmth and strength seeped into every cell of her body. The light was so strong that she could no longer see his image, only a shimmering mist. A sense of love overwhelmed her.

She lay down and slept. Awaking later, she was pleased that she was still in the beautiful garden. Wondering if she had dreamed about the man in the robes, she sat up. She was no longer naked but dressed in a thin long white dress. Her feet were bare. A man with short dark hair sat by the river with his back to her; he appeared to be fishing. Dressed in black shorts his body was fit and muscular, tanned dark brown from the sun. Without turning he patted the side of the grass next to him. He seemed to want her to join him. The ground felt cool like silk under her feet as she walked over to him. Sitting next to him, she rested her head onto his shoulder and he took her hand in his. His hands were large, smooth and familiar as was his scent. Indigo felt safe and secure; closing her eyes sleep overcame her once more.

Awaking properly, Indigo stared into the darkness. She smiled. The dream told her that she was on the right path. The higher powers were pleased with her progress. All was well in her world.

To follow: *Indigo's life is transformed...*

Lightning Source UK Ltd.
Milton Keynes UK
UKOW06f1805260715

255832UK00005B/55/P